UNDERSTANDING STUDENT DISCIPLINE
IN CALIFORNIA SCHOOLS

A PARENT'S GUIDE TO GENERAL AND SPECIAL EDUCATION DISCIPLINE

Dora Dome, Esq

© 2017 Dora Dome Law

Copyright © 2017 by Dora Dome Law

All rights reserved. When forms or sample documents are included, their use is authorized only by educators, school districts, school sites, and noncommercial entities who have purchased the book. Except for that usage, no part of this book may be reproduced or utilized in any form or by any means, electronic or mechanical, including photocopying, recording, or by any information storage and retrieval system, without permission in writing from the author.

The information contained in this book is general guidance on the implications of the laws covered and best practice protocols in implementing those laws. The information is not legal advice and should not take the place of seeking legal advice from legal counsel on specific issues. Any forms provided in this book are provided as sample guidance and should be reviewed to ensure that they are consistent with district policy and subsequent legal amendments.

Cover Design by Ryan Brockmeier for Two Seven Eight Media
Layout Design by Taisha Rucker, Esq.
Reviewed by Erin Scott, Esq.

ISBN-13: 978-1545146590
ISBN-10: 1545146594

Contents

Foreword by Richard Ruderman
Supporting Parent Access To Laws Governing Student Discipline in California _____ vii

Dedication _____ viii

About the Author _____ ix

◆ ◆ ◆

Introduction _____ 11

◆ ◆ ◆

Part I: Student Discipline — 12

Chapter 1   Student Suspensions _____ 13
    Other Means of Correction
      When Other Means of Correction Are Required
      When Other Means of Correction Are Not Required
    Suspension Generally
      Definition – What it is and what it isn't…
      Class Suspensions
      School Suspensions
      Suspension Due Process
      Legal Standard to Suspend
      Jurisdiction to Suspend - 48900(s)
    A Little Bit About Bullying
      Sexual Harassment
      Hate Violence
      Harassment, Threats, Intimidation

Chapter 2   Expulsion Recommendations _____ 22
    Expulsion Due Process
    Mandatory Expulsion Recommendations – Education Code 48915(c)
      Possession Of A Firearm
      Brandishing A Knife
      Selling A Controlled Substance

    Sexual Battery
      Misdemeanor Sexual Battery
      Felony Sexual Battery
    Sexual Assault
      Rape; "Duress;" "Menace"
      Inducing Consent To Sexual Act By Fraud Or Fear
      Sodomy
      Lewd Or Lascivious Acts Involving Children
      Oral Copulation
      Penetration By Foreign Object
    Possession of an Explosive
   Discretionary Expulsion Recommendations – Education Code 48915(a)
    Secondary Findings Required To Support Discretionary Expulsion Recommendations
   Stipulated Expulsion Recommendations

Chapter 3 Expulsion Hearings 33

   Expulsion Hearing Procedural requirements
   School Board Hearing Or Administrative Panel Hearing
   Authority of The Administrative Panel
   The Expulsion Packet
   Burden of Proof, Hearsay, And Direct Evidence
   Sworn Declaration Process – "Fear Declaration" – 48918(f)(2)
   Authority Of The School Board

Chapter 4 Expulsion Orders 41

   Discretionary Offenses
   Mandatory Offenses
  Suspended Enforcement Of The Expulsion Order
  Notice Of Decision To Expel
  Educational Options During Expulsion
  Readmission

Chapter 5 County Appeal of Expulsion Order 45

  Standard For County To Review An Expulsion Order
  Decision Of The County Board

Chapter 6 Who Gets Notice of Education Code Violations 48

   Mandatory Reporting to Law Enforcement
   Notification to Teachers

Part II: Special Education Discipline 50

| Chapter 7 | Services During Short Term Suspensions | 51 |
| Chapter 8 | Manifestation Determination Procedures | 53 |

    Change in Placement - Removal For More than 10 Consecutive School Days
    Change in Placement - Series of Removals That Constitute A Pattern
    Manifestation Determination IEP

| Chapter 9 | IDEA Special Circumstances - 45 -Day Placements | 56 |
| Chapter 10 | Disciplinary Appeals | 58 |

    Procedures
    Authority of the Hearing Officer

| Chapter 11 | Protections for Children Not Yet Eligible for Special Education | 60 |

    Is The District Deemed to Have Knowledge?
    When A Basis of Knowledge Exists
    Exceptions To There Being a Basis of Knowledge
    When There is Not A Basis of Knowledge

Appendix 63

A.	2017 California Education Code Section 48900	64
B.	2017 California Education Code Section 48900.5	68
C.	2017 California Education Code Section 48915	70
D.	Glossary of Relevant Disciplinary Definitions	73
E.	Sample - Student Statement Form	75
F.	Sample - Sworn Declaration - Fear	76
G.	Sample - Notice of Suspension	77
H.	Sample – Letter Extending Suspension Pending Expulsion	79
I.	Sample – Letter Extending Suspension Pending Expulsion – IDEA	81

J.	Sample – Letter Terminating Expulsion Recommendation - IDEA	83
K.	Sample - Expulsion Packet Checklist	84
L.	Sample - Expulsion Packet Table of Contents	85
M.	Sample – Stipulation and Waiver of Expulsion Hearing	86
N.	Special Education Discipline Regulations – 34 CFR 300.530 – 537	89
	n1 CFR 300.530 Authority of school personnel	90
	n2 CFR 300.531 Determination of setting	94
	n3 CFR 300.532 Appeal	95
	n4 CFR 300.533 Placement during appeals	98
	n5 CFR 300.534 Protections for children not determined eligible for special education	99
	n6 CFR 300.535 Referral to and action by law enforcement and judicial authorities	102
	n7 CFR 300.536 Change of placement because of disciplinary removals	104
	n8 CFR 300.537 State enforcement mechanisms	106

Foreword
Supporting Parent Access To Laws Governing Student Discipline in California

Dora Dome's book "Understanding Student Discipline in California Schools" is an excellent handbook and guide for parents seeking a better understanding of the laws governing disciplinary procedures in California schools. Parents who are dealing with the school system can easily be overwhelmed by the disciplinary process. The school discipline process is particularly difficult for parents because they typically are also struggling with the emotional turmoil of wanting to help their child while understanding and coping with the consequences of the child's conduct. At the same time, there is also the question of whether the school system made the right call. There are often multiple sides to the same story. Dora Dome's book will greatly assist any parent caught up in this process.

The book is not just a great guide for parents, it is also useful for educators, advocates, and attorneys. It provides an excellent overview of the school disciplinary process.

The school disciplinary process serves multiple purposes. School officials need to maintain safe schools. Parents and students are entitled to a fair hearing. Students who commit serious infractions should face appropriate consequences. However, the ultimate goal of the process is to reform the student who commits the infraction and return the student to the educational system.

Education is a fundamental right. The law is also intended to protect students who are wrongfully accused of misconduct, which sadly does occur. I've been involved in many such cases.

As an attorney representing families of children with special needs for over twenty years, I have seen firsthand the stress and impact on families of the discipline process. It is critical for parents to fully understand their rights. It is also essential for all parties, parents and school officials, to carefully and objectively gather and analyze the facts related to the incident that gave rise to discipline. Emotions often run high on both sides of the equation.

At the end of the day, these cases most often come down to objective problem-solving to lay out an appropriate plan for the student subject to discipline. This is one of the reasons I greatly appreciate Dora's work. Although we have worked on opposite sides of the table in cases involving student discipline, Dora was always a great problem-solver and worked collaboratively to come up with common sense solutions.

Lastly, for any parent whose child faces the most serious disciplinary consequence of expulsion, I strongly recommend that you seek out an attorney familiar with the student discipline process for legal guidance and representation.

Richard Ruderman
Ruderman & Knox, LLP
1300 National Drive, Suite 120
Sacramento, CA 95834

Dedication

This book is dedicated to all parents who have children in the California public schools and have found themselves in need of assistance navigating the school discipline process. I have represented school districts in the area of student issues, including special education and student discipline, for over 20 years. What has become increasing clear to me is that in order to ensure that the rights of students are protected, all the folks involved in the student discipline process; parents, teachers, and administrators, need to have a better understanding of the student discipline process, with all its nuances and opportunities to exercise discretion, with the objective of keeping children engaged in school and learning from their misbehaviors. Unfortunately, there are very few resources available that provide parents with a clear understanding of the discipline process.

There is also the very real fact that many families are unable to access the legal supports and services that could assist them in addressing the complicated discipline issue that they may encounter. This book was written with you in mind. My intention is that this book will provide clarification and guidance in these complicated discipline situation and allow you to feel knowledgeable and empowered when advocating for the rights of your child.

Dora Dome
2017

About the Author

Dora J. Dome, Esq.

Dora J. Dome has practiced Education Law for over 20 years, primarily in the areas of student issues and special education. In April 2016, she published her first book, ***Student Discipline, Special Education Discipline, Anti-Bullying and Other Relevant Student Issues: A Guide For Practitioners***, which has been described as a "**must-have**" for anyone seeking to understand student discipline and bullying. She graduated from University of Hawaii, Richardson School of Law (J.D.) and from University of California, Los Angeles (B.A.).

She currently provides legal representation to school districts on student issues, and has renewed her emphasis on developing and conducting professional development trainings for district staff that focus on Bullying and Legal Compliance, viewed through an Equity Lens, in a proactive effort to build staff capacity to address the changing needs of their students.

Ms. Dome's work with Bullying focuses on helping school districts create the necessary infrastructure to identify and address bullying in schools and to provide staff with effective strategies to respond to various forms of bullying and harassment. Ms. Dome's legal compliance trainings provide up-to-date information and guidance on how to 'stay legal' in the areas of Special Education, Student Discipline, Counseling and Mandated Reporting, Sexual Harassment, Discriminatory Harassment and Section 504.

Admitted to the Hawaii State Bar in 1996, Ms. Dome served as a special education consultant and trainer for the Hawaii State Department of Education and Hawaii State Department of Health for five years. Ms. Dome was admitted to the California Bar in 2003. She worked with the education law firm of Dannis Woliver Kelley, (fka Miller Brown and Dannis) for eight years.

Ms. Dome has studied in the areas of Race and Ethnicity, Critical Legal Studies and Critical Race Theory and has been certified as a Cultural Diversity Trainer by the National Coalition Building Institute (aka NCBI). She has developed and conducted trainings for numerous school districts and school boards in the areas of student diversity and equity, student and special education discipline, harassment/discrimination, bullying, special education, No Child Left Behind, alternative assessments for African American students, Section 504, and student records.

Ms. Dome also regularly presents at association conferences such as ACSA, CSBA and CASCWA. She participated on the Gay & Lesbian Athletics Foundations (aka GLAF) Keynote Panel on "Race and Racism in LGBT Athletics" and presented at the NCAA Black Coaches Association Annual Conference on "Homophobia in Sports."

Ms. Dome is a Lecturer at the University of California at Berkeley, teaching Education Law and Policy in Principal Leadership Institute (PLI) Program. She was also an Adjunct Professor at Mills College teaching in the administrative credential program for soon to be administrators.

Introduction

School children engage in conduct that could potentially subject them to varying forms of school discipline on a daily basis. The nature of the discipline can range from a referral for informal counseling with an administrator or staff person to a recommendation for expulsion from the district, and will be determined by the severity of the conduct. The disciplinary code of conduct governing student conduct in school can be found in the California Education Code (hereinafter referred to as "CA Ed. Code") at 48900, et seq. (See Appendix A - 2017 version of California's disciplinary code.)

It is imperative that parents, and anyone who advocates for the rights of students, understand the rights of the student so that they can advocate on their behalf. To that end, it is my hope that this book will provide parents, and anyone involved in the student discipline process, with a useful, easy to understand, step-by-step guide to student discipline. Where appropriate, I will provide citations to relevant sections of the CA Ed. Code for your reference. Additionally, here is a link to the California Legislative website, where you can search all California Laws, including the CA Ed. Code, by citation or keyword: http://leginfo.legislature.ca.gov/faces/codes.xhtml.

Part I

Student Discipline

Student Suspensions

When a student engages in a minor rule violation, and redirection is not effective, the school's response will typically be a referral to the school administrator or counselor to discuss the misbehavior and appropriate alternative responses or conduct. Once they have completed their discussion, the student will be allowed to return to the class. The reason for the referral and the intervention should be documented in the school's student information system, either in the student's disciplinary or intervention tracker. This record is maintained throughout a student's K-12 education and is accessible to you as part of your child's student record.

When the misconduct involves more serious rule violations, the student may face consequences such as, a requirement to write an age appropriate paper about the impact of the conduct, a behavior contract, detention, trash duty, Saturday school, a class or school suspension, or a recommendation for expulsion, to name a few. As part of, or instead of disciplinary action, the school may require a student to perform community service on school grounds or, with written permission of the parent or guardian, off school grounds during the student's non-school hours. (CA Ed. Code 48900.6) You should ask your child's school for a list of their progressive discipline options and practices.

You should also be aware that schools will sometimes remove students "informally" from their class for various behaviors and place the student in another class for the remainder of the class period. The law allows for this to happen once every five days. (CA Ed Code 48925(d)(3)) To the extent that some schools may engage in this practice more frequently than once every five days, the student is experiencing what we call a "de facto" suspension. The school is not recording the removals as a suspension, which often means that the parent is not being informed of the removals. This practice is a violation of your child's rights and you should ask your school's administrator if they utilize this practice with your child and, if so, how frequently.

The law **encourages** schools to provide alternatives to suspension or expulsion that are age appropriate and designed to address and correct the student's specific misbehavior. (CA Ed. Code 48900(v)) Additionally, the law **requires** that schools first utilize other means of correction prior to suspending a student from school, in most situations. (CA Ed. Code 48900.5 – See Appendix B – 2017 Version of California's list of "other means of correction") Lastly, when addressing students who are truant, tardy, or otherwise absent from school activities, it is the intent of the Legislature that alternatives to suspension or expulsion be imposed. (CA Ed. Code 48900(w)) Therefore, schools should not suspend students as a consequence for missing school and are encouraged to work with parents to understand the underlying reasons for the lack of attendance, or the barriers that inhibit attendance, and create a plan designed to improve the student's attendance.

Other Means of Correction

When Other Means of Correction Are Required

In an effort to reduce the overuse of exclusionary discipline for all students, and in particular students of color and other marginalized groups who experience disproportionate levels of exclusionary discipline, CA Ed. Code 48900.5 requires that there must be evidence documented by the school that "other means of correction" have failed to bring about proper conduct prior to suspending a student, including when the student is suspended but attending school in supervised suspension classroom.

CA Ed. Code 48900.5 provides a non-exhaustive list of examples of "other means of correction" to provide guidance and clarification to parents and educators about the potential tools that could be utilized in the school's efforts to respond to and correct student misbehavior. An examination of the list makes it clear that "other means of correction" does not include progressive discipline that is punitive in nature. There are a number of school districts that have incorporated many of these strategies into their discipline matrix. Yet, there are many more that still need to identify available strategies and support school sites in the implementation of alternative means of addressing student misbehavior.

Exclusionary discipline should rarely be the first recourse. Teachers and administrators are encouraged to consider how the proposed disciplinary consequences are designed to change the misbehavior or help the student make better choices. If the teacher or administrator is unable to articulate how the proposed consequence will help change the student's behavior or help the student make better choices, it should be considered whether the proposed consequence is appropriate or whether something else should be done in addition to the proposed consequence. Punishment, by itself, does not improve student behavior or conduct and should rarely be administered in isolation.

When Other Means of Correction Are Not Required

CA Ed. Code 48900.5 allows administrators to exercise their discretion and consider suspension upon a first offense (no requirement of other means of correction) when specific conditions are met. A student, including an individual with exceptional needs, as defined in Section 56026, may be suspended, subject to certain procedural protections, for any of the reasons listed in Section CA Ed. Code 48900 upon a first offense, if the principal or superintendent of schools determines that the pupil violated subdivision (a), (b), (c), (d), or (e) of Section 48900 or that the pupil's presence causes a danger to others. (See Appendix A for the 2017 definitions of these offenses) However, just because the school can suspend on a first offense for some conduct violations, does not always mean it should. It is important for administrators to always consider whether exclusionary discipline is necessary for safety reasons or whether it will change the student's behavior and it is important for parents to understand the discretion that an administrator possesses and encourage her/him to exercise it. If exclusionary discipline is not necessary for safety reasons, then it would be appropriate for the administrator to consider alternatives to excluding the student.

Suspension Generally

The first question you should ask is "what offense(s) has your child been charged with?" At the time of suspension, the school is legally required to make a reasonable effort to contact the student's parent in person or by telephone. If your child is suspended from school, you must be notified in writing of the suspension. (CA Ed. Code 48911(d)) This written notification is typically called a "Notice of Suspension" and will state the CA Ed. Code 48900 section(s) that allegedly has been violated. (See Appendix G – Sample Notice of Suspension)

Once you have identified the CA Ed. Code section(s) that has been violated, your next move should be to have the administrator provide you with a description of the conduct your child engaged in. Beyond the verbal summary of the administrator, there should be written statements by the alleged victim, if any, and witnesses describing the incident. You are entitled to redacted copies of any statements describing the incident that have identifiable information about your child and are maintained by the school and the copies, or the right to inspect the documents, **must** be provided within five business days of your request for the records. (CA Ed. Code 49069) A redacted copy means that the names of minors other than your child that appear in the document have been removed to protect their identity. (See Appendix E – Sample Witness Statement Form)

Suspension Definition - What it is...

CA Ed. Code 48925(d) defines suspension as removal of a pupil from ongoing instruction for adjustment purposes.
- No student may be suspended from school for more than five consecutive days for any single act of misconduct.
- A student's suspension may be extended beyond five days only pending a

recommendation for expulsion.
- A student may not be suspended from school for more than twenty (20) cumulative days in the school year.
- A student may be suspended for an additional ten (10) days for reassignment or adjustment purposes. When a student transfers mid-year into a new school district, it is up to the new district whether or not to begin counting days of suspension from the number of days suspended in the previous district or to start over.

What it isn't…

"Suspension" **does not mean** any of the following:

(1) Reassignment to another education program or class at the same school where the pupil will receive continuing instruction for the length of day prescribed by the governing board for pupils of the same grade level.

A pupil who is reassigned to another class, at the same grade level, and continues to receive instruction is not suspended.

(2) Referral to a certificated employee designated by the principal to advise pupils.

A pupil who is referred to an administrator or counselor, etc., for the purpose of discussing the appropriateness of the pupil's behavior, **who is allowed to return to the class from which the referral came following the discussion**, is not suspended.

(3) Removal from the class, but without reassignment to another class or program, for the remainder of the class period without sending the pupil to the principal or the principal's designee as provided in Section 48910. Removal from a particular class shall not occur more than once every five schooldays.

A pupil who is referred to a "buddy classroom" for the remainder of the class period as a timeout or other intervention, is not suspended. However, this type of removal can only occur once every five schooldays. To the extent this strategy is utilized more frequently than once every five days, it would be considered a suspension and, potentially, a violation of the pupil's civil rights.

Class Suspensions

Teachers may suspend your child from their class for any act listed in CA Ed. Code 48900 for the remainder of the day of suspension and the next day. When a teacher suspends your child from her/his class, there are certain steps that must be taken:

1. The teacher **must** immediately report the suspension to the principal and send the student to the principal or designee for appropriate action.

2. As soon as possible, the teacher **must** ask the parent to attend a parent-teacher conference regarding the suspension.
3. If practicable, a school counselor or school psychologist **may** attend.
4. A school administrator **must** attend the conference if the teacher or parent so requests.
5. The student shall not be returned to the class from which s/he was suspended, during the period of suspension, without the agreement of the teacher of the class and the Principal.
6. A student suspended from a class cannot be placed in another regular class during the period of suspension. However, if the student has more than one class per day, the student will attend her/his other classes.
7. The teacher may refer the student to the Principal for consideration of a suspension from the school.
(CA Ed. Code 48910)

School Suspensions

Similar to teacher suspensions from class, the principal or designee may suspend your child from school for any of the reasons listed in CA Ed. Code 48900, subject to the limitations stated in CA Ed. Code 48900.5, for no more than five consecutive school days. (CA Ed. Code 48911(a)) (See Exhibit A & B)

Suspension - Due Process

Prior to suspending your child from school, the principal or designee must provide your child with due process. The principal or designee must hold an informal conference with your child, where s/he is informed of the reason for the disciplinary action and the evidence against her/him, and given the opportunity to present her/his version and evidence in her/his defense. (CA Ed. Code 48911(b)). The administrator is not required to contact or notify you prior to holding this meeting with the student. The administrator may suspend your child without the informal conference if an "emergency situation" exists. The informal conference must be held within two days following the emergency situation, unless your child waives her/his right to the conference or is physically unable to attend for any reason, including incarceration or hospitalization. (CA Ed. Code 48911(c)).
Parents are required to respond without delay to a request from school officials to attend a conference regarding her/his child's behavior. (CA Ed. Code 48911(f)).

Legal Standard to Suspend

If your child has engaged in conduct that has lead to a suspension from school, be aware that the "burden of proof" required before suspending your child from school is a "preponderance of the evidence," which is interpreted to mean your child "more likely than not" engaged in the conduct for which s/he is being charged.

There is no specific mention of burden of proof in the Education Code or underlying legal authority. The best practice for an administrator charged with deciding whether to suspend a pupil is to be convinced by a preponderance of the available evidence that suspension is justified and appropriate after meeting with the student, presenting the student with the evidence against her/him, and soliciting the student's version of the facts.

Jurisdiction to Suspend - 48900(s)

In order for a school to suspend your child, it must have jurisdiction over your child at the time s/he committed the offense. A school district has jurisdiction to discipline your child for conduct violations. The act must be related to a school activity or school attendance occurring within a school under the jurisdiction of the superintendent of the school district or principal, or occurring within any other school district. Your child may be suspended or expelled for acts that are enumerated in 48900 et seq. and **related to a school activity or school attendance that occur at any time**, including, but not limited to, any of the following:
    (1) While on school grounds.
    (2) While going to or coming from school.
    (3) During the lunch period whether on or off the campus.
    (4) During, or while going to or coming from, a school-sponsored activity.

Note that the jurisdictional statement described above does NOT apply to expulsion recommendations based on CA Ed. Code 48915. See Chapter 2 -Expulsion Recommendations for the applicable jurisdictional statement.

A Little Bit About Bullying

Bullying is a term that is widely used, with individuals attributing many different meanings to the word. It is used to refer to the conduct of a first grade boy who pulls the hair of a female classmate, to the conduct of a high school student who calls another student a derogatory name every time she sees that student, and everything in between. Many of the nationally available anti-bullying programs often describe bullying conduct as being "repeated over time," and involving an "imbalance of power."

While these are often characteristics of bullying, it is important for parents, administrators and school staff to understand that California has a legal definition of bullying that does not require the conduct be "repeated over time," or involve an "imbalance of power." Therefore, it is imperative that you understand the elements of California's "bullying" definition and the conduct that violates it, in order to advocate for your child.

CA Ed. Code Section 48900(r) defines bullying as:
- **Severe** or **pervasive physical** or **verbal** act or conduct, including communications made in writing or by means of an electronic act, and including one or more of the following:

- o Sex Harassment (48900.2)
- o Hate Violence (48900.3)
- o Threats, harassment, intimidation (48900.4)
- Has or is reasonably predicted to have one or more of the following:
  - o Reasonable pupil in fear of <u>harm to person or property</u>
  - o Reasonable pupil to experience <u>substantially detrimental effect to physical or mental health</u>
  - o Reasonable pupil to experience <u>substantial interference with academic performance</u>
  - o Reasonable pupil to experience <u>substantial interference with ability to participate in or benefit from services, activities, or privileges provided by the school</u>

Breaking this definition down into its three main sections will help you better understand its elements.

<u>First Section</u>

- **Severe** <u>or</u> **pervasive physical** <u>or</u> **verbal** act or conduct, including communications made in <u>writing</u> or by means of an <u>electronic act</u>

The first section of the bullying definition describes the severity and nature of the bullying conduct. The use of the word "severe" suggests that the bullying conduct only needs to happen once, and if the conduct is severe enough, it would be sufficient to constitute bullying as defined in law. The bullying conduct can be physical, verbal, written or electronic. So, the first step in determining whether your child's conduct amounts to bullying, is to understand the severity and nature of the conduct.

If the conduct is electronic, then the conduct is considered cyber-bullying. Cyber-bullying is the creation or transmission **originated on or off the schoolsite**, by means of an electronic device, including, but not limited to, a telephone, wireless telephone, or other wireless communication device, computer, or pager, of a communication, including, but not limited to, a message, text, sound, image, or a post on a social network internet web site. Cyber-bullying is bullying by an electronic act and all of the elements of the Bullying definition must be established just as if the bullying had occurred in person.

<u>Second Section</u>

… including one or more of the following:
- o Sex Harassment (48900.2)
- o Hate Violence (48900.3)
- o Threats, harassment, intimidation (48900.4)

The second section of the bullying definition requires that the bullying conduct violate one of these three existing sections in the CA Ed. Code. Specifically, it means that in California, for the underlying conduct to be considered bullying, it must be in the form of "Sexual Harassment," "Hate Violence," or "Threats, Harassment or Intimidation."

CA Ed. Code defines each of the above sections as follows:

§48900.2 – Sexual Harassment
Unwelcome sexual advances, requests for sexual favors, and other verbal, visual, or physical conduct of a sexual nature, made by someone from or in the work or educational setting that is considered by a reasonable person of the same gender as the victim to be sufficiently severe or pervasive to have a negative impact upon the individual's academic performance or to create an intimidating, hostile, or offensive educational environment.

§48900.3 – Hate Violence
Caused, attempted to cause, threatened to cause, or participated in an act of hate violence. (Hate violence is violence directed toward an individual based on that person's membership to protected class. i.e. disability, gender, gender identity, gender expression, nationality, race or ethnicity, religion, sexual orientation, or association with a person or group with one or more of these actual or perceived characteristics.)

§48900.4 – Harassment, Threats, Intimidation
The pupil has intentionally engaged in harassment, threats, or intimidation, directed against school district personnel or pupils, that is sufficiently severe or pervasive to have the actual and reasonably expected effect of materially disrupting classwork, creating substantial disorder, and invading the rights of either school personnel or pupils by creating an intimidating or hostile educational environment.

So, the second step in determining whether your child's conduct amounts to bullying, is to examine the conduct and determine whether it meets the elements of one of the three definitions above. If your child's conduct does not meet all of the elements of one of the three sections above, the conduct is not "bullying" under California Law and your child can't be disciplined for Bullying. However, just because your child's conduct does not meet the bullying definition, does not mean your child can't be disciplined for the misbehavior. It does mean that the administrator would need to identify the appropriate CA Ed. Code section, if applicable, in order to discipline your child.

Be aware that "Sexual Harassment," "Hate Violence," or "Threats, Harassment or Intimidation" are also independent sections of the CA Ed. Code and, simultaneously, subsections of the Bullying definition. As independent sections of the CA Ed. Code, these sections only apply to students in grades 4-12. However, as a subsection of the Bullying definition, the California Department of Education ("CDE") has interpreted these sections to apply to all grades, K-12.

Practically, this means that if your child is a third grader who is being charged with bullying based on conduct that amounts to sexual harassment, your child can be suspended for bullying in violation of 48900(r), but your child could not be legally charged with 48900.2 - sexual harassment, due to the grade restrictions that apply to sexual harassment.

However, if your child is an eighth grader being charged with bullying based on conduct that amounts to sexual harassment, your child must be charged with both Bullying - 48900(r) and 48900.2 - sexual harassment. This is because any student grade 4-12 who violates the Bullying statute 48900(r), is by definition also violating either 48900.2 – Sexual Harassment, 48900.3 – Hate Violence, or 48900.4 – Threats, Harassment, or Intimidation.

Third Section

- Has or is reasonably predicted to have one or more of the following:
    - Reasonable pupil in fear of harm to person or property
    - Reasonable pupil to experience substantially detrimental effect to physical or mental health
    - Reasonable pupil to experience substantial interference with academic performance
    - Reasonable pupil to experience substantial interference with ability to participate in or benefit from services, activities, or privileges provided by the school

The third and final section of the Bullying definition examines the impact that the bullying conduct had or could have reasonably been predicted to have on a "reasonable person," which often times is the victim.

Therefore, the final step in determining whether your child's conduct amounts to bullying, is to examine the impact of the conduct on a "reasonable person" and determine whether any of the negative impacts listed have occurred or could have reasonably been predicted to occur.

CA Ed. Code 48900(r)(3) defines "reasonable pupil" as a pupil, including, but not limited to, an exceptional needs pupil, who exercises average care, skill, and judgment in conduct for a person of his or her age, or for a person of his or her age with his or her exceptional needs. While it is arguable whether there is really such a thing as a "reasonable pupil," administrators are expected to consider what would be a reasonable response based on the severity and nature of your child's conduct, as well as the characteristics of the victim.

Expulsion Recommendations

The CA Ed. Code is structured such that it presents the basic disciplinary code of conduct first in section 48900. CA Ed. Code Section 48915 then details more severe instances of conduct listed in 48900, that if violated, create an increased health or safety hazard for a school such that an expulsion recommendation may be appropriate. There are three types of expulsion recommendations: mandatory, discretionary, and stipulated.

As a practical matter, a recommendation for expulsion should only be made when the law requires it, pursuant to CA Ed. Code 48915(c) – Mandatory Expulsion Recommendations, or when the conduct is so severe that maintaining the student on campus safely is impractical.

Expulsion – Due Process

Once your child has been recommended for expulsion, your child's right to due process is again triggered. When your child was only facing a one to five day suspension, her/his due process consisted of an informal conference with the administrator as described in Chapter 1. However, because the expulsion recommendation proposes to take away a significant right of your child, to attend district schools for up to one calendar year, the amount of process that is due to your child increases significantly.

First, the school administrator has the right to extend your child's suspension, beyond the initial five days, pending the expulsion decision by the district's governing board. (CA Ed. Code 48911(g)) This means that your child may be suspended from school for thirty (30) school days or longer, until the governing board makes a decision about the expulsion recommendation. (CA Ed. Code 48918(a)(1)) However, prior to extending your child's suspension pending expulsion, the school administrator must invite you and your child to a meeting to discuss the expulsion recommendation. If this meeting does not occur prior to the expiration of the five day suspension for the same conduct, your child would have the right to return to school on day six and remain until the extension of suspension conference is held. Before the administrator can extend your child's suspension, s/he **must** determine that allowing your child to remain at school during the pendency of the expulsion process would <u>cause a danger to persons or property or a threat of disrupting the instructional process</u>. (CA Ed. Code 48911(g))

If the determination is made to extend your child's suspension pending the outcome of the expulsion process, your child may not attend her/his school, or any school events or activities on any campus within the district. During the period of suspension, the law does not require the district to provide your child with educational services. However, <u>you should check the policies and practices of your district to determine if it will provide any educational support for your child during this time.</u> The school must provide you with written notice of its decision to extend your child's suspension pending expulsion. (See Appendix H - Letter Extending Suspension Pending Expulsion & Appendix I - Letter Extending Suspension Pending Expulsion – IDEA.)

If your child is a foster child, her/his attorney and an appropriate representative of the county child welfare agency must be invited to participate in the extension of suspension meeting. Second, your child has a right to a due process hearing to contest the allegations against her/him. These rights and process will be described more fully in Chapter 3 – Expulsion Hearing.

Mandatory Expulsion Recommendations – Education Code 48915(c)

There are only five (5) offenses that require a mandatory recommendation for expulsion. If your child engages in one of the five offenses, your child must be suspended and recommended for expulsion. If the governing board finds that there is "substantial evidence" establishing that your child engaged in the conduct, the governing board must expel her/him. Those five offenses include:

1. Verified possession of a firearm;

   It is important to know what distinguishes a "firearm" from an "imitation firearm," as possession of an imitation firearm does not require a mandatory recommendation for expulsion.

   California Penal Code 165210 defines "firearm" as "a device, designed to be used as a weapon, from which is expelled through a barrel, a projectile by the force of an explosion or other form of combustion." Therefore, the determining characteristic is whether the weapon uses an explosion or combustion to propel the projectile. If "yes," it is a firearm, requiring a mandatory recommendation for expulsion. If "no," the weapon is an imitation firearm, which does not require a mandatory recommendation for expulsion and would require "secondary findings" to support an expulsion recommendation. (See Discretionary Expulsions for a description of "secondary findings")

2. Brandishing a knife at another person;

   Education Code 48915(g), defines a knife as "… any dirk, dagger, or other weapon with a fixed, sharpened blade fitted primarily for stabbing, a weapon with a blade fitted primarily for stabbing, a weapon with a blade longer than 3 1/2 inches, a folding knife with a blade that locks into place, or a razor with an unguarded blade."

Be aware that California Penal Code 626.10 definition of knife includes a knife with a blade longer than 2½ inches. Therefore, law enforcement may consider a weapon a knife based on Penal Code, when the weapon, in fact, does not meet the California Education Code definition of a knife.

If a school is pursuing an expulsion recommendation based on possession or brandishing a knife, it is imperative that there is evidence that the weapon used meets the 48915(g) definition of a knife. You, as an advocate for your child, should be clear how and if the weapon meets the definition of a knife.

Example:

Student brandishes what the school believes to be a knife. The school pursues a mandatory recommendation for expulsion based on brandishing a knife but the administrator has not specified what characteristics make the weapon a knife. The administrator enters a photo of the knife into evidence during the expulsion hearing. When the characteristics of the knife are examined, it is determined that it does not meet the definition of a knife and the student cannot be expelled for brandishing a knife.

Even though the weapon is called a knife, the school administrator must examine it and determine what characteristics make it a knife, such as the length of the blade or the fact that the blade locks into place. If the weapon does not meet the definition of a knife, the student can still be expelled, however the expulsion recommendation would have to be based on possession of a dangerous object and on the fact that "due to the nature of the act," brandishing the knife at another student, the student's presence on campus is a danger to the student or others. (CA Ed. Code 48915(a)(1)(ii)) These additional charges must have been charged at the same time as the brandishing charge for the case to go forward.

3. Selling a controlled substance;

   Selling any amount of a controlled substance requires a mandatory recommendation for expulsion.

   Examples:

   A student sells hits off his marijuana pipe for $1 per hit. Even though the amount is relatively miniscule, the conduct would require a mandatory recommendation for expulsion.

A student has a prescription for Adderall. The student sells her Adderall to another student for $5 per pill. The fact that the student has a legal prescription for the controlled substance does not protect her from an expulsion recommendation for selling a controlled substance.

4. Sexual assault or sexual battery;

CA Ed. Code Sections 48900(n) and 48915(d) designate conduct that amounts to a sexual battery or sexual assault as a mandatory recommendation for expulsion. However, rather than define the terms, the CA Ed. Code references relevant California Penal Code Sections for definitions of the conduct.

If your child is facing an expulsion recommendation based on sexual battery or sexual assault, you should request that the administrator identify the relevant Penal Code sections the conduct violates and you should be clear what the elements are of the offense that the school must prove to support a decision to expel your child.

Sexual Battery

There are two types of sexual battery that commonly occur on school campuses, one is a misdemeanor and one is a felony. This distinction is not relevant, as both fall under CA Ed. Code 48900(n) and are subject to a mandatory recommendation for expulsion. However, being aware of the distinction between the two types of sexual battery helps to understand the evidence necessary to prove the two offenses.

<u>Misdemeanor Sexual Battery – California Penal Code 243.4(e)(1)</u>

When looking at the definition of any offense, it is useful to think about the definition in terms of elements that must be proved to support an expulsion order. A misdemeanor sexual battery has three elements: 1) touching an intimate part of another person, 2) if the touching is against the will of the person touched, and 3) is for the **specific** purpose of sexual arousal, sexual gratification, or sexual abuse.

<u>Intimate Part</u>

An "intimate part" is defined by Penal Code to be "the sexual organ, anus, groin, or buttocks of any person, and the breast of a female." So, there must be evidence that an intimate part was touched.

Against The Will of The Person Touched

This element is self-explanatory. The victim did not consent to the touching.

Specific Purpose - Sexual arousal, Sexual gratification, or Sexual abuse

The general standard to determine intent for sexual battery crimes is to look to "[A] defendant's statement of his intent and by the circumstances surrounding the commission of the act.. . . In objectively assessing a defendant's state of mind during an encounter with a victim, the trier of fact may draw inferences from his conduct, including any words the defendant has spoken. . ."People v. Craig (1994) 25 Cal.App.4th 1593, 1597.

Sexual Arousal or Gratification

To prove "arousal" and "gratification" in reported California cases on sexual battery, the substantial evidence must support a finding that the act was committed for the purposes of sexual pleasure.

Facts that could support a finding of sexual arousal or gratification of the perpetrator include a male with an erection, exposing himself, or masturbating or attempting sexual arousal of the victim by touching the victim's intimate places or forcing the victim to touch the perpetrator in intimate places. People v. Dixon, 75 Cal.App.4th. 935.

Sexual Abuse

"Sexual abuse" needs to be shown by a battery on another person's "intimate part" done either to harm or humiliate that person. Therefore, it is an "either /or" element of the offense. Sexual abuse cases satisfy this element with facts showing intent to hurt or humiliate, which appear to arise more often with school-age students.

A juvenile court conviction of a 14-year-old minor male defendant who pinched the breast of a 16-year-old female victim was upheld with findings that the assault caused her emotional distress and resulted in a significant bruise. In re Shannon T., 50 Cal.Rptr.3d at 565, 567. The court found that the defendant inflicted a sexual battery under § 243.4(e) with the specific purpose of sexual abuse because he first told her, "Get off the phone. You're my ho," and when the victim responded, "Whatever," and walked away, the defendant pursued her, slapped her face, grabbed her arm, and pinched her breast. Id. at 566–67.

Similarly, the court found the minor defendant committed sexual battery when he poked the center of the victim's buttocks, penetrating about an inch. Because the defendant laughed with his companions as he touched the victim and used derogatory language, the court found the evidence demonstrated the defendant's purpose was sexual abuse. In re A.B., 2011 WL 193402, at *1.

Lastly, a middle school student, who slapped his classmate-victim "with an open hand in her crotch area" was guilty of misdemeanor sexual abuse under Penal Code section 243.4(e)(1). The juvenile offender blamed his friends for telling him to do it. The record showed that the victim was "mad, embarrassed, and 'kind of scared" and chased the defendant, who "ran away laughing." These facts led the court to conclude that the defendant "understood that his action would embarrass and humiliate" the victim. In re Carlos C., 2012 WL 925029 (Cal.Ct.App.2012)

These are examples of the factual evidence the school would need to prove to establish that your child's intent in engaging in the conduct was sexual arousal, sexual gratification or sexual abuse.

Felony Sexual Battery – California Penal Code 243.4(a)

A felony sexual battery has four elements, 1) Touching an intimate part of another person, 2) while that person is unlawfully restrained by the accused or an accomplice, and, 3) if the touching is against the will of the person touched and, 4) is for the purpose of sexual arousal, sexual gratification, or sexual abuse.

As compared to a misdemeanor sexual battery, a felony sexual battery requires that the victim be unlawfully restrained and there is no requirement to establish "specific intent," only "intent."

To prove a felony sexual battery, there must be evidence of all four elements.

Unlawfully Restrained

The person must be "unlawfully restrained" during the touching. The general rule is that a person is "unlawfully restrained when his or her liberty is being controlled by words, acts or authority of the perpetrator aimed at depriving the person's liberty." People v. Pahl, (1991) 226 Cal.App.3d 1651,1661. Effectively blocking or impeding any exit the victim could take could also be considered "unlawful restraint."

See Misdemeanor Sexual Battery (above) for a more detailed analysis of the other three elements of a felony sexual battery. Although the analysis in the sexual arousal, gratification or abuse section is specifically addressing "specific intent," which is an element of a misdemeanor sexual battery, evidence that supports a finding of "specific intent" would also support a finding of "intent" in a felony battery case.

Sexual Assault

If your child allegedly commits or attempts to commit a sexual assault, s/he is subject to a mandatory recommendation for expulsion. It is important for parents to understand that there are six (6) different offenses that are considered sexual assaults pursuant to CA Ed. Code and you must be clear which offense is being alleged to have been violated. Below are the six offenses that are sexual assaults, however, the definitions are not complete and you MUST refer to the relevant Penal Code ("PC") sections for a comprehensive definition.

PC 261. Rape; "Duress;" "Menace"

(a) Rape is an act of sexual intercourse accomplished with a person not the spouse of the perpetrator, under any of the following circumstances: (See PC for circumstances.)

PC 266c. Inducing consent to sexual act by fraud or fear

Every person who induces any other person to engage in sexual intercourse, sexual penetration, oral copulation, or sodomy when his or her consent is procured by false or fraudulent representation or pretense that is made with the intent to create fear, and which does induce fear, and that would cause a reasonable person in like circumstances to act contrary to the person's free will, and does cause the victim to so act. (See PC for comprehensive definition.)

PC 286. Sodomy

(a) Sodomy is sexual conduct consisting of contact between the penis of one person and the anus of another person. Any sexual penetration, however slight, is sufficient to complete the crime of sodomy. (See PC for comprehensive definition.)

PC 288. Lewd or lascivious acts involving children

(a) Except as provided in subdivision (i), any person who willfully and lewdly commits any lewd or lascivious act, including any of the acts constituting other crimes provided for in Part 1, upon or with the body, or any part or member thereof, of a child who is under the age of 14 years, with the intent of arousing, appealing to, or gratifying the lust, passions, or sexual desires of that person or the child. (See PC for comprehensive definition.)

PC 288a. Oral copulation

(a) Oral copulation is the act of copulating the mouth of one person with the sexual organ or anus of another person. (See PC for comprehensive definition.)

PC 289. Penetration by foreign object

(a) (1) (A) Any person who commits an act of sexual penetration when the act is accomplished against the victim's will by means of force, violence, duress, menace, or fear of immediate and unlawful bodily injury on the victim or another person. (See PC for comprehensive definition.)

5. Possession of an explosive.

   Under CA Ed. Code Section 48915, subdivision (h), "the term 'explosive' means 'destructive device' as described in Section 921 of Title 18 of the United States Code." Under this statute, a "destructive device" means "(A) any explosive, incendiary, or poison gas; bomb; grenade; rocket having a propellant charge of more than four ounces; missile having an explosive or incendiary charge of more than one-quarter ounce; mine, or device similar to any of the devices described in the preceding clauses." 18 U.S.C. § 921(a)(4)(A).

   Common denominators to the above examples of "destructive devices" are that they are weapons that are actually capable of harm by way of explosion or flammability, with the possible exception of "poison gas." The common definition of "explode" involves bursting violently, expanding with force, and projecting outwards.

   Example

   A student put a "chemical mixture" in a plastic bottle, which was thrown, kicked, or rolled into a group of students at a crowded assembly. The contents exploded in some fashion, with the cap remaining on the bottle. No one was injured. There were no flames, although some reported smoke. This may have been mist. The school cannot prove it was smoke. The school must determine whether the object constitutes an explosive device, for purposes of determining whether a recommendation of expulsion is mandatory under California Education Code section 48915(c).

   An explosive device is by definition a destructive weapon, and it appears the school would not have any evidence that the "chemical mixture" in the bottle was destructive or a weapon. Therefore, with the facts given, there does not appear to be sufficient evidence to prove the bottle was an explosive device. If the District could prove that the substance in the bottle was flammable or poisonous, it would be an explosive device. If the weapon does not meet the definition of an explosive, the student can still be expelled. However, the expulsion recommendation would have to be based on possession of a dangerous object and the fact that "due to the nature of the act," throwing a devise that exploded in the middle of a crowded assembly, the student's presence on campus is a danger to the student or others. (Ed Code 48915(a)(1)(ii))

These are the only offenses that <u>require</u> that your child be recommended for expulsion.

Also note that the conduct listed in 48915(c) must occur at school or **at a school activity off school grounds** in order for the district to have jurisdiction to recommend an expulsion based on this section. Therefore, if your child engages in conduct that violates any of the above CA Ed. Code sections, the conduct MUST have occurred at school or at a school activity off school grounds in order for the school to have jurisdiction to discipline your child under this section. This is a more limited jurisdiction than what applies to 48900 violations.

Lastly, the school administrator only needs to prove that your child engaged in the conduct charged in order to support a mandatory expulsion recommendation. (See Appendix C for the 2017 version of the CA Ed Code 48915(c) offenses.)

Discretionary Expulsion Recommendations - Education Code 48915(a)

School administrators have discretion to suspend or expel for all conduct violations, <u>except the five listed in 48915(c)</u>, and discussed above. In light of the data clearly establishing the overuse of exclusionary discipline for all students and, particularly the disproportionate impact of exclusionary discipline on students of color and other marginalized groups, it is important that administrators exercise their significant discretion and understand that just because they can suspend or expel does not mean that they should.

CA Ed. Code 48915(a) lists the following conduct violations that may lead to a recommendation for expulsion: causing serious physical injury to another person not in self-defense; possession of a knife or other dangerous object; possession of a controlled substance (with exceptions); robbery or extortion; and assault or battery on a school employee. However, if the principal or designee determines that expulsion should not be recommended under the circumstances or that an alternative means of correction would address the conduct, a recommendation for expulsion should not be made for these conduct violations.

The idea that students who engage in the above listed behaviors would not be recommended for expulsion represents a shift from the practice of strictly enforcing zero tolerance policies. This shift has been embraced and supported by the state legislature in the form of legal amendments clarifying what constitutes "other means of correction," limitations added to 48900(k) removals, and clarification of conduct that does and does not violate 48915 offenses.

Also note that the conduct listed in 48915(a) must occur **at school or at a school activity off**

school grounds in order for the district to have jurisdiction to recommend an expulsion based on this section. This is a more limited jurisdiction than what applies to 48900 violations.

Your child may also be subjected to a discretionary recommendation for expulsion for any CA Ed. Code 48900 offense, except 48900(t) – Aiding and abetting, if the school administrator determines that secondary findings exist. However, all 48900 expulsion recommendations are subject to the broader jurisdictional statement in 48900(s).

Secondary Findings Required To Support Discretionary Expulsion Recommendations

If your child is facing a discretionary expulsion recommendation, in addition to proving that your child engaged in the underlying offense, the administrator must also prove one or both of the following, 1) "Other means of correction" are not feasible or have failed to bring about proper conduct; or 2) "Due to the nature of the violation," the presence of your child causes a continuing danger to the physical safety of the pupil or others. (CA Ed Code 48915(b)(1) & (2); 48915(e)(1) & (2))

Examples of the type of evidence that would prove "other means of correction," can be found at 48900.5. In order to prove "due to the nature of the violation," the administrator would need to introduce evidence that looked specifically at the conduct for which your child is facing the expulsion recommendation and demonstrate how engaging in the conduct created a danger for your child or others.

For example, a student gets into a fight with another student and beats the student so badly that the student must be hospitalized for serious injuries. If the administrator also produced evidence that teachers attempted to deescalate the student and he ignored their directives and, in fact, began physically attacking the teachers, this evidence could support a finding that due to the nature of the act, the student's presence is a danger.

Evidence of both the underlying CA Ed. Code violation and the relevant secondary finding is required to support a discretionary recommendation for expulsion. (See Appendix C for the 2017 version of the CA Ed Code 48915(a) offenses.)

Stipulated Expulsion Recommendations

A stipulated expulsion is basically a process that allows your child to admit guilt and waive her/his right to an expulsion hearing. This is a useful process when your child is not contesting the facts of the conduct violation and has admitted to engaging in the conduct. The value of a stipulated expulsion is that it allows for the expulsion process to be expedited, thus allowing your child to be placed in the alternative setting sooner and minimizing the academic impact of the missed instruction.

There is no statutory authority for stipulated expulsions. The validity of the process was upheld in Choplin v. Conejo Valley Unified School District, 903 F.Supp. 1377 (C.D. CA 1995). The case held that a person may waive a constitutional right if it can be established by clear and convincing evidence that the waiver is voluntary, knowing and intelligent and, specifically, that parents may waive the right to a pre-expulsion hearing and consent to discipline.

If your district uses the stipulated expulsion process, it is important that the stipulation that you and your child sign clearly delineates the conduct violations your child is admitting to, including the secondary findings, and the rights that your child is waiving by signing the stipulation. The stipulation should be signed by both you and your child, and appropriate school personnel. (See Appendix M - Sample Stipulation and Waiver of Expulsion Hearing.)

Expulsion Hearings

If your child is being recommended for expulsion, it is imperative that you understand the applicable rules and procedures in order to protect the rights of your child. School administrators in most school districts are responsible for presenting the expulsion case. The process has many procedural requirements that implicate legal concepts, such as due process, rules of evidence, and burden of proof. It is important that parents and advocates understand how to navigate the expulsion process to ensure that the law is followed and that the rights of the student are protected.

Generally speaking, the expulsion hearing should follow fairly common steps. The chair of the hearing body or the expulsion hearing facilitator will read a script that identifies your child and the charges against her/him. They will identify the date and location of the hearing and introduce the members of the hearing body and summarize the hearing process. Typically, both sides are given the opportunity to provided "Opening Statements." The purpose of the opening statement is to summarize each party's position and the evidence which it intends to present to support that position. The opening statements are not evidence and there is no discussion of the opening remarks.

Following the opening statements, the District will present its witnesses and evidence. After each witness' testimony, you or your child's representative may cross-examine the witness. Reexamination and re-cross-examination is often permitted. At the end of direct and cross-examination, members of the hearing body may ask clarifying questions.

After the school has concluded its case, you or your representative may present testimony and exhibits. After your direct examination of each of your witnesses, the school will have the opportunity to cross-examine your witness, members of the hearing body may ask clarifying questions. Either side may present rebuttal evidence. After all the evidence has been submitted, each party will have the opportunity to make a closing statement. These closing statements summarize each party's position and request that the hearing body reach the conclusion in favor of the party.

Expulsion Hearing Procedural Requirements

CA Ed. Code 48918 lists the procedural requirements applicable to expulsion hearings. These procedural requirements must be adhered to in order to ensure that your child receives her/his due process rights.

While not exhaustive, below is a list of some of the relevant procedural requirements to keep in mind as the expulsion hearing process moves forward. For a comprehensive list of the rules governing expulsion procedures, refer to CA Ed. Code 48918.

- The expulsion hearing is to be held within 30 school days after the date that the principal or the superintendent determines that your child has committed any act in violation of § 48900, unless you request, in writing, that the hearing be postponed. (CA Ed. Code § 48918(a)(1))
- Your child is entitled to one postponement of the expulsion hearing (for any reason), for a period of not more than thirty (30) calendar days. (CA Ed. Code § 48918(a)(1))
- Notice of the hearing must be provided to family at least 10 days prior to the hearing. (CA Ed. Code § 48918(b))
- Your child has the right to be represented by counsel or a non-attorney advisor. (CA Ed. Code 48918(b)(5))
- Your child has the right to inspect and obtain copies of all documents to be used at the hearing. (CA Ed. Code 48918(b)(5))
- Your child has the right to confront and question all witnesses who testify at the hearing. (CA Ed. Code 48918(b)(5))
- Your child has the right to question all other evidence presented. (CA Ed. Code 48918(b)(5))
- Your child has the right to present oral and documentary evidence on her/his behalf, including witnesses. (CA Ed. Code 48918(b)(5))

If your child is a foster child and the recommended expulsion is discretionary, notice of the expulsion hearing **must** be provided to your foster child's attorney and an appropriate representative of the county child welfare agency at least ten (10) calendar days before the date of the hearing. (CA Ed. Code 48918.1(a)(1)) If your foster child is facing a mandatory recommendation for expulsion, the school **may** provide notice of the expulsion hearing as described above. (CA Ed. Code 48918.1(a)(2))

School Board Hearing Or Administrative Panel Hearing

The law requires the School Board to conduct the expulsion hearing in a session closed to the public, unless you request, in writing, at least five (5) days prior to the date of the hearing, that the hearing be conducted at a public meeting. (CA Ed. Code 48918(c)(1)) Instead of conducting the hearing itself, the School Board may designate a hearing officer or appoint an impartial administrative panel ("Panel") to conduct the hearing. (CA Ed. Code 48918(d))

In most districts, particularly larger districts with a large number of expulsion hearings, the School Board appoints a Panel to conduct the hearing. The Panel must consist of three or more certificated persons, none of whom is a member of the School Board or employed on the staff of the school where your child is enrolled. (CA Ed. Code 48918(d))

Authority of the Administrative Panel

In districts where a Panel conducts the expulsion hearing, they act as the School Board's fact finders and, within three days after the hearing, they must decide whether to recommend the expulsion of your child to the School Board. If the Panel decides not to recommend your child's expulsion, the expulsion proceedings must be terminated and your child must be immediately reinstated and permitted to return to the classroom instructional program from which the referral was made, unless you request another placement in writing. (CA Ed Code 48918(e))

Historically, if the Panel found that there was "substantial evidence" to support the expulsion recommendation, it was required to recommend the student's expulsion to the School Board and it was up to the School Board to decide whether to order the expulsion. However, recent amendments have extended the Panel's authority to decide not to recommend the expulsion of a student who it has found to have committed a Mandatory 48915(c) offense. In this situation, the student must be reinstated and may be referred back to her/his prior school, another comprehensive school, or involuntarily transferred to a continuation school in the district. (CA Ed. Code 48918(d))

In either case, the decision of the Panel not to expel is final and does not progress to the School Board.

If the Panel recommends your child's expulsion, it must draft findings of fact in support of its recommendation to be submitted to the School Board for its consideration. The Panel's findings must be based solely on the evidence presented at the expulsion hearing. (CA Ed. Code 48918(f)(1))

The Expulsion Packet

Once the investigation has been completed and it has been determined that the expulsion recommendation for your child will go forward, the administrator will gather all the evidence and create the expulsion packet. Below is a list of the items that are typically included in an expulsion packet.

- Notice of Suspension
- Principal's Recommendation for Expulsion

- Notice of Meeting to Consider Extension of Suspension
- Notice of Extension of Suspension
- Notice of Hearing Date and Charge Letter (notice)
- Incident reports/witness statements (redacted)
- Physical evidence (weapon, drugs, photos, etc.)
- Interventions and discipline tracker
- Teacher reports/ transcripts/attendance
- Any other relevant documents (e.g. continuance request, police report, "fear" declaration, etc.)

As the parent supporting your child in the expulsion process, there are a few items to pay close attention to. First, ensure that the charges listed in the Notice of Hearing are accurate. The Notice of Hearing is the official list of Education Code violations and the school may only proceed at the expulsion hearing on the charges listed in the Notice of Hearing. If the Notice of Hearing lists multiple CA Ed Code section violations, the school will be required to introduce evidence to prove all of the elements for each of the sections charged.

Second, if witness statements are part of the expulsion packet to be introduced at the hearing, check the dates the statements were written to understand whether they were written contemporaneously with the incident. When the statements were written could potentially be used to determine authenticity and/or credibility and could go to the weight the hearing body gives the document in the hearing.

Third, make sure any photos of physical evidence that are introduced at the expulsion hearing depict what they were intended to show. For instance, if a picture of a knife is being introduced to establish that the weapon meets the definition of a knife based on the length of the blade, the photo should have a ruler next to the blade establishing that the blade is longer than 3 ½ inches. Make sure the school administrator clearly identifies how the weapon meets the definition of a knife. Additionally, if you need any equipment to introduce demonstrative evidence, such as audio or video equipment, contact the district prior to the hearing and verify that they can make the equipment available for the expulsion hearing. If they do not have access to equipment you need, be prepared to bring your own.

Lastly, if the case has been continued beyond the statutory timelines for any reason, the expulsion packet must include documentation supporting the continuance.

While the CA Ed. Code does not require that the expulsion packet be provided to you prior to the hearing, best practice is for the school to provide a copy of the expulsion packet as soon as it is available, in order to give you and your child an opportunity to review the evidence to be presented and prepare a defense. (See Appendix K – Sample Expulsion Packet Checklist & Appendix L – Sample Expulsion Packet Table of Contents)

Burden of Proof, Hearsay, And Direct Evidence

The burden of proof required to support an expulsion order is "substantial evidence." This means that the administrator presenting the case must present evidence that "a reasonable mind could accept as adequate to support a conclusion" that the student engaged in the conduct charged.

Additionally, CA Ed. Code states that an expulsion order may not be based solely on "hearsay." Hearsay, in a school disciplinary case, is a statement made outside of the expulsion hearing, that is offered in the hearing, by someone other than the declarant, as evidence to prove the truth of the matter asserted. For example, all written witness statements are hearsay because they are statements written outside of the expulsion hearing, that are being offered in the hearing, by someone other than the person who wrote the statement, and they are being offered for their truth regarding the information described in the statement.

Hearsay may be introduced in an expulsion hearing. However, there must also be "direct evidence" to support an expulsion order. Direct evidence is evidence offered at the hearing by someone with firsthand knowledge of the incident. Therefore, in addition to written witness statements, there must be a "warm body" testifying at the hearing from firsthand knowledge of the incident.

If your child admits to the charged conduct violation in a written statement, her/his admission is not hearsay and the written admission can be relied upon, as direct evidence, to support an expulsion order. The question is whether the admission addresses the conduct violation directly. For instance, if your child writes, "I did it," that has very little value in proving the school's case, as it is vague as to what your child is admitting to doing. If your child instead writes, "I sold weed to Tom at school on Monday," that admission could be relied upon to support the expulsion order for selling a controlled substance, even if no one physically testifies at the hearing. The written admission is direct evidence. Additionally, the administrator's testimony at the hearing that your child admitted verbally to the same administrator that s/he sold weed to Tom at school on Monday would also be admitted as direct evidence.

Once the administrator has completed presenting her/his case, you and your child will have the opportunity to present a defense to the allegations. At this time, you may call witnesses on your behalf to offer "relevant" evidence regarding the allegations against your child. "Relevant" evidence is defined by CA Ed. Code as, "…the kind of evidence upon which reasonable persons are accustomed to rely in the conduct of serious affairs." (CA Ed. Code 48918(h)(1))

You may also offer "character" evidence in the form of witness testimony or documents.

"Character" evidence is commonly introduced to show a student's character or disposition and is often used to make a case for leniency or compassion.

Your child also has the right to testify on her/his behalf or not to testify. If your child chooses to testify, s/he will be required to answer questions on cross-examination by the school following her/his direct testimony. Your child would be required to answer the cross-examination questions or risk having the entirety of her/his testimony stricken from the record.

Any testimony provided by your child in an expulsion hearing is expressly deemed to be a privileged communication protected by subdivision (b) of Section 47 of the Civil Code. (CA Ed. Code 48918.6)

Your child also has the constitutional right not to testify under the Fifth Amendment of the Constitution. If your child chooses to exercise her/his right not to testify, the hearing body cannot hold her/his refusal against her/him nor can it presume that s/he engaged in the conduct charged as a result of refusing to testify.

Sworn Declaration Process – "Fear Declaration" – 48918(f)(2)

Due to the CA Ed. Code's requirement that there be some "direct evidence" to support an expulsion recommendation, districts often encounter the situation where there is a witness to the conduct violation, the witness has written an incident statement (which is hearsay), yet the witness is unwilling to testify.

In this situation, it is the administrator's responsibility to determine why the witness is unwilling to testify. If it is because the witness does not want to be involved or does not want to "snitch," and the administrator needs the witness' testimony to support the expulsion recommendation, then the administrator would need to find a way to encourage the witness to participate in the process or the expulsion hearing cannot go forward.

However, if testifying at the hearing would cause an <u>unreasonable risk of psychological or physical harm</u> to the witness, the CA Ed. Code allows for the witness to testify via sworn declaration. This means that the witness' incident statement could be admitted into evidence as "direct evidence," an exception to the hearsay rule, and relied upon to support an expulsion order.

The first step is for the administrator to document what the unreasonable risk of psychological or physical harm is. The documentation could be a written statement by the witness that your child has a reputation for violence and has threatened to harm the witness in the past. The documentation could also be evidence that since the incident, the witness suffered severe anxiety which has manifested in the form of loss of appetite, insomnia, school anxiety, or lowered academic performance. This fear declaration should be separate from the witness' underlying incident statement documenting the conduct violation.

Once the facts supporting a finding of an unreasonable risk of psychological or physical harm have been stated and documented, the documentation of the fear declaration must be made part of the expulsion packet to be considered during the hearing. At some point during the expulsion hearing, the administrator must request that the School Board or the Panel (whichever body is hearing the case) consider the fear declaration and make a determination regarding whether there is an unreasonable risk of psychological or physical harm if the witness is forced to testify. Your child has the right to refute the evidence and argue that an unreasonable risk of psychological or physical harm does not exist. At the conclusion of the arguments, the hearing body must make a determination either way.

If the hearing body determines that there **is not** an unreasonable risk of psychological or physical harm, the witness' underlying incident statement may be admitted into evidence, but only as hearsay, and it cannot be relied on solely as a basis to support an expulsion order against your child. However, if the hearing body determines that there **is** an unreasonable risk of psychological or physical harm, the witness' underlying witness statement may be admitted into evidence as "direct" evidence, and may be relied on as the only evidence to support an expulsion order against your child.

The hearing body must clearly state on the record its findings and specifically identify the written incident statement it is admitting as direct evidence. It is important to note that the value of this process is dependent on the content of the underlying written incident statement, because only what is written in that statement will be admitted into evidence as direct evidence. For instance, if the underlying written incident statement says, "I saw Tom do it," the introduction of that observation does not prove the conduct violation. If, instead, the underlying written incident statement says, "I saw Tom tackle Bob from behind and begin punching him in the head," this observation goes directly to proving the conduct violation. (See Appendix F for a Sample "Fear" Declaration)

Authority of the School Board

Whether the expulsion hearing is conducted by the School Board or the Panel, the final action to expel your child can only be taken by the School Board in a public session. (CA Ed. Code 48918(j)) Typically, the School Board will assign a number to your child's case for posting on the public agenda. Your child's name will never be used either on the Board's agenda or in public session, unless you have made a written request for the hearing to be in public session.

When the School Board receives a recommendation to expel for a mandatory violation, whether in the form of a Panel recommendation or a Stipulation signed by you and your child, if the School Board agrees that there is substantial evidence to support the expulsion recommendation, the School Board must expel your child. (CA Ed. Code 48915(d)) If your child has admitted to the conduct violation(s), there is, by definition, substantial evidence that your child engaged in the conduct charged.

If the School Board receives a recommendation to expel for a <u>discretionary</u> violation, whether in the form of a Panel recommendation or a Stipulation signed by you and your child, it always has the discretion to choose to expel or not to expel, even if the School Board believes that your child engaged in the charged conduct. (CA Ed. Code 48915(b))

Expulsion Orders

Discretionary Offenses

If your child is expelled for a discretionary act, the School Board must set a date for your child to be reviewed for readmission no later than the last day of the semester following the semester in which the expulsion occurred. If the expulsion is ordered during the summer session or the intersession period of a year-round program, the School Board must set a date, not later than the last day of the semester following the summer session or intersession period in which the expulsion occurred, when your child must be reviewed for readmission. (CA Ed. Code 48916(a))

Mandatory Offenses

If your child has been expelled for a mandatory act, pursuant to 48915(c), the School Board must set the review for readmission date one year from the date the expulsion occurred. However, the School Board may set an earlier date to review your child's readmission on a case-by-case basis. (CA Ed. Code 48916(a))

The School Board must also recommend a plan of rehabilitation for your child at the time of the expulsion order, which may include, but not be limited to, periodic review as well as assessment at the time of review for readmission. The plan may also include recommendations for improved academic performance, tutoring, special education assessments, job training, counseling, employment, community service, or other rehabilitative programs. (CA Ed. Code 48916(b))

If your child is expelled for reasons relating to controlled substances, or alcohol, the School Board may require your child, prior to returning to school, to enroll in a county-supported drug rehabilitation program. However, your child cannot be required to enroll in a rehabilitation program pursuant to this section without your consent. (CA Ed. Code 48916.5)

You must also be provided with a description of the readmission procedure at the time the expulsion order is entered. (CA Ed. Code 48916(c))

Suspended Enforcement Of The Expulsion Order

If the School Board decides to expel your child, they may also decide to suspend the enforcement of the expulsion order for a period of not more than one calendar year. During the period of the suspension of the expulsion order, your child is considered to be on probationary status. (CA Ed. Code 48917(a) & (c))

As a condition of the suspension of enforcement, your child may be assign to a school, class, or program that is deemed appropriate for her/his rehabilitation. The rehabilitation program to which your child is assigned may provide for your involvement in your child's education in ways that are specified in the rehabilitation program. However, your refusal to participate in the rehabilitation program cannot not be considered by the School Board in determining whether your child has satisfactorily completed the rehabilitation program. (CA Ed. Code 48917(a))

The School Board may revoke the suspension of an expulsion order under this section if your child commits any 48900 violation or violates any of the district's rules and regulations governing pupil conduct. When the School Board revokes the suspension of an expulsion order, your child may be expelled under the terms of the original expulsion order. (CA Ed. Code 48917(d))

If your child satisfactory completes the rehabilitation plan, the School Board must reinstate your child in a school of the district and _may_ also order the expungement of any or all records of the expulsion proceedings. (CA Ed. Code 48917(e))

Be aware that a decision of the School Board to suspend the enforcement of an expulsion order does not affect the time period and requirements for the filing of an appeal of the expulsion order with the county board of education required under Section 48919. (See Chapter 5 - County Appeal Of An Expulsion Order for discussion of process below)

Notice of Decision To Expel

The district must send you a written notice of any decision to expel or to suspend the enforcement of an expulsion order during a period of probation and the notice must include all of the following:

    (1) Notice of your right to appeal the expulsion to the county board of education.
    (2) Notice of the education alternative placement to be provided to your child during the time of expulsion.
    (3) Notice of your and your child's obligation under subdivision (b) of Section 48915.1, upon your child's enrollment in a new school district, to inform that school district of your child's expulsion. (CA Ed. Code 48918(j))

Educational Options During Expulsion

If the School Board expels your child, it must refer your child to a program of study that meets all of the following conditions:

(1) Is appropriately prepared to accommodate pupils who exhibit discipline problems.
(2) Is not provided at a comprehensive middle, junior, or senior high school, or at any elementary school.
(3) Is not housed at the schoolsite attended by the pupil at the time of suspension. (CA Ed. Code 58915(d))

In many situations, the educational placement available to an expelled student is provided through the County in its Community Day School Program ("CDS"). However, many districts have a CDS or Alternative School option within the district. You would need to check with your district to determine what types of programs were available.

If your child is expelled from your school district for an act other than a 48915 (a) or (c) violation, you may request enrollment in another school district where you have either established legal residence or have an inter-district agreement. (CA Ed. Code 48915.1(a)) You **must** inform the new district of your child's status as an expelled student with the previous school district. (CA Ed. Code 48915.1(b))

The School Board of the new school district may make a determination to deny enrollment to your child, after a hearing, if it determines that your child poses a potential danger to either the pupils or employees of the new school district. (CA Ed. Code 48915.1(c))

The School Board of the new school district may consider the following options when making its determination whether to enroll your child:

(1) Deny enrollment.
(2) Permit enrollment.
(3) Permit conditional enrollment in a regular school program or another educational program. (CA Ed. Code 48915.1(d))

If the School Board of the new district determines that your child does not pose a danger to either the pupils or employees of the school district, it must permit your child to enroll in a school in the school district during the term of the expulsion. (CA Ed. Code 48915.1(e))

If your child is expelled from your school district for an act listed in 48915 (a) or (c), s/he is not allowed to enroll in any other school or school district during the period of expulsion unless it is a county community school pursuant to subdivision (c) of Section 1981, or a juvenile court school, as described in Section 48645.1, or a community day school pursuant to Article 3 (commencing with Section 48660) of Chapter 4 of Part 27. (CA Ed. Code 48915.2)

Readmission

At the conclusion of the expulsion period, you may apply for your child's readmission into the district. The School Board must readmit your child, unless they find that your child has not met the conditions of the rehabilitation plan or continues to pose a danger to campus safety or to other pupils or employees of the school district. (CA Ed. Code 48916(c))

If the School Board denies your child's readmission they must make a determination either to continue your child's the placement in the alternative educational program initially selected for your child during the period of the expulsion order or to place your child in another program that may include, but need not be limited to, serving expelled pupils, including placement in a county community school. (CA Ed. Code 48916(d))

The School Board must provide you and your child with written notice describing the reasons for denying your child's readmittance into the regular school district program. The written notice shall also include the determination of the educational program for your child. Your child must enroll in that educational program unless you choose to enroll your child in another school district. (CA Ed. Code 48916(e))

County Appeal of Expulsion Order

If your child is expelled from school, you may file an appeal to the county board of education within 30 calendar days following the decision of the governing board to expel. If you do not file your appeal within the 30 calendar day timeline, you will loss your right to appeal the expulsion order of the district School Board and its decision will be final. The county board of education must hold the hearing within 20 schooldays following the filing of your formal request. (CA Ed. Code 48919)

The county board of education will consider the record of the hearing before the district governing board, together with such applicable documentation or regulations as may be ordered, when rendering its decision. No evidence other than that contained in the record of the proceedings of the district School Board may be heard unless the county board grants a new hearing as provided in Section 48923. (CA Ed. Code 48921)

It is your responsibility to submit a written transcription of the expulsion hearing for review by the county board. You would provide the school district with a copy of your County Appeal and request that it create a transcript of the expulsion hearing.

You must pay the cost of the transcript unless either of the following situations exists:

(1) Where the pupil's parent or guardian certifies to the school district that he or she cannot reasonably afford the cost of the transcript because of limited income or exceptional necessary expenses, or both.

(2) In a case in which the county board reverses the decision of the local governing board, the county board shall require that the local board reimburse the pupil for the cost of such transcription. (CA Ed. Code 48921)

Standard For County To Review An Expulsion Order

In order for the county board of education to accept your appeal of your child's expulsion order, the reason for the appeal must fall under one of four categories. The review by the county board of education of the decision of the district School Board is limited to the following questions:

(1) Whether the School Board acted without or in excess of its jurisdiction.

A proceeding without or in excess of jurisdiction includes, but is not limited to, a situation where an <u>expulsion hearing is not commenced within the time periods</u> prescribed by this article, a situation where an <u>expulsion order is not based upon the acts enumerated in Section 48900</u>, or a <u>situation involving acts not related to school activity or attendance</u>.

(2) Whether there was a fair hearing before the School Board.

(3) Whether there was a prejudicial abuse of discretion in the hearing.

An abuse of discretion is established in any of the following situations:
- If school officials have not met the procedural requirements of this article.
- If the decision to expel a pupil is not supported by the findings prescribed   b y Section 48915.
- If the findings are not supported by the evidence.

A county board of education may not reverse the decision of a governing board to expel a pupil based upon a finding of an abuse of discretion unless the county board of education also determines that the abuse of discretion was prejudicial

(1) Whether there is relevant and material evidence which, in the exercise of reasonable diligence, could not have been produced or which was improperly excluded at the hearing before the governing board.

Therefore, when you file your appeal to the county board of education, you must frame your issues consistent with one of the four questions above or the county office of Education will refuse your appeal.

Decision Of The County Board

If the county board finds that relevant and material evidence exists which, in the exercise of reasonable diligence, could not have been produced or which was improperly excluded at the hearing before the district School Board, it may do either of the following:

(1) Remand the matter to district School Board for reconsideration and may in addition order your child reinstated pending the reconsideration.

(2) Grant a new hearing upon reasonable notice thereof to you and to the district School

Board. The hearing shall be conducted in conformance with the rules and regulations adopted by the county board under Section 48919. (CA Ed. Code 48923(a))

If the county board determines that the decision of the district School Board is not supported by the findings required to be made by Section 48915, but evidence supporting the required findings exists in the record of the proceedings, the county board shall remand the matter to the governing board for adoption of the required findings. This remand for the adoption and inclusion of the required findings will not result in an additional hearing. However, the final action to expel your child based on the revised findings of fact shall meet all requirements of subdivisions (j) and (k) of Section 48918. (CA Ed. Code 48923(b))

In all other cases, the county board shall enter an order either affirming or reversing the decision of the district School Board. In any case in which the county board enters a decision reversing the local board, the county board may direct the local board to expunge the record of your child and the records of the district of any references to the expulsion action and the expulsion shall be deemed not to have occurred. (CA Ed. Code 48923(c))

Who Gets Notice of Education Code Violations

Over the past few years the "school-to-prison pipeline" has become an issue championed by groups across the political spectrum. The concern arises because, over the past ten to twenty years, schools across the country have increasingly involved law enforcement in incidents involving pupils which, in earlier years, would have been managed internally within the school through its own disciplinary system. Various causes of this increased criminalization of student behavior have been identified, but much of it has resulted from "zero tolerance" policies following tragic and extreme incidents such as the Columbine High School shooting. These "zero tolerance" policies have resulted in severe discipline, and even arrests, for innocent behaviors as districts abandoned the ability to apply common sense and to view incidents in their proper contexts.

Although there is no legal mandate or directive that California schools report, or not report, any crimes not covered by Section 48902, schools are encouraged to adopt policies that balance the need to evaluate individual incidents to determine whether there is a need to involve law enforcement with the danger that such discretion can result, intentionally or not, in disparate negative impact on certain racial and socio-economic groups. Failure to assure equitable application of policies theoretically could result in litigation alleging discrimination, lack of equal protection and/or due process violations

Mandatory Reporting to Law Enforcement

There are certain situations where the school must report your child's conduct to law enforcement. CA Ed. Code 48902 sets out which crimes a school district must report to law enforcement. These include assaults with deadly weapons, assaults with sufficient force likely to cause severe bodily injury, incidents involving the use, sale, possession, and distribution of illegal substances, alcohol, or imitation substances, and incidents involving a firearm or possession of explosives. Failure to report these crimes is an infraction and, conversely, reports made in good faith cannot result in civil liability.

If the school informs you that it intends to report your child to law enforcement, you should as the administrator if it is an offense that requires reporting to law enforcement and, if not, ask the administrator to consider not reporting the incident to law enforcement to avoid unnecessarily criminalizing your child.

Notification to Teachers

Be aware that CA Ed. Code 49079(a) requires a school district to inform the teacher of each pupil who has engaged in, or is reasonably suspected to have engaged in, a conduct violation listed in 48900, except possession or use of tobacco or nicotine products. The district must provide the information to the teacher based upon any records that the district maintains in its ordinary course of business, or receives from a law enforcement agency, regarding a pupil described in this section.

Any information received by a teacher pursuant to this section shall be received in confidence for the limited purpose for which it was provided and shall not be further disseminated by the teacher. The same information must be provided to the current teachers of any student who was suspended or expelled in another district and subsequently transfers into a new school district.

Part II

Special Education Discipline

7

Services During Short Term Suspension

If your child is a child with a disability under the Individuals with Disabilities in Education Act ("IDEA") or Section 504 of the Rehabilitation Act of 1973 ("Section 504"), your child is entitled to certain procedural protections when certain conditions are met. (See Appendix N for the rules that apply to special education discipline)

As a basic rule, a student with special needs is subject to the same grounds for suspension and expulsion that apply to students without disabilities. The basic difference between the discipline of a student with special needs and a general education student is that a student with special needs is entitled to certain procedural protections throughout the disciplinary process and when a change of placement is being contemplated.

If your child has an Individual Educational Plan ("IEP"), s/he will be treated the same as a general education student during the first ten (10) cumulative days of suspension. This means that your child with special needs is not entitled to IDEA protections for short term suspensions, until the eleventh (11th) school day of removal. An IEP team can decide to proactively hold an IEP meeting to examine the behavior leading to the short term suspensions during the first ten days, but the IDEA does not require such a meeting as part of the disciplinary procedural protections.

When your child with special needs under IDEA is suspended for more than 10 cumulative school days in a school year, s/he is entitled to continue to receive services, during the periods of suspension beyond ten days. For instance, a student with special needs under IDEA has already been suspended for 9 cumulative days this school year and has engaged in a conduct violation for which she is going to be suspended for an additional 5 days. The additional 5 days will bring the student's cumulative suspensions for the year to 14 days. IDEA requires that starting on day 11 through day 14, the student receive services while suspended.

The services provided to the student during these four days must 1) enable the student to participate in the general curriculum; and 2) allow the student to make progress toward meeting the goals in the student's IEP. The student is not entitled to identical services to what she would have received if she were in school. The more services the student receives in her IEP, the more services she might need while suspended to meet the standard articulated above. For example, if the student was receiving resource services one hour per day, she might only need two total hours of home instruction during the four days in order to meet the legal standard. However, if she were in a self-contained Special Day Class with many other supports and services, the services she might need during the four day suspension to meet the legal standard may be one to two hours each of the four days. <u>What those services will be during the short term suspension will be determined by appropriate school personnel in consultation with the teacher, and should be documented in the IEP and sent home to the parents of the student</u>. Your consent or approval is not required in determining the services your child will receive during a short-term removal.

Students with Section 504 Plans are not entitled to educational services during short term suspensions.

IDEA requires the principal or designee to monitor the number of days, **including portions of days**, that students with a valid IEP have been suspended during the school year to determine when the procedural protections are triggered and the students' right to services during suspension begins.

Manifestation Determination Procedures

Another disciplinary procedural safeguard provided by the IDEA is the requirement to conduct a manifestation determination IEP within 10 school days of any decision to **change the placement** of your child with a disability because of a violation of a code of student conduct. It is important to remember that the requirement to conduct a manifestation determination IEP when there is a proposed change in placement also applies to students with 504 Plans.

It is the decision to change your child's placement that triggers the requirement to conduct a manifestation determination IEP. Therefore, it is important to understand what proposed actions constitute a change in placement. IDEA defines a "change in placement" as either 1) a removal for more than 10 consecutive school days, or 2) a series of removals that constitute a pattern.

Change in Placement - Removal for More than 10 Consecutive School Days

In California, the only way there can be a change in placement of your child with special needs based on a removal for more than 10 consecutive school days in the school year, is if s/he is being recommended for expulsion or s/he is facing a 45-day removal pursuant to IDEA special circumstances.   In both instances, once the decision has been made to change your child's placement, the requirement to conduct a manifestation determination is triggered.

Change in Placement - Series of Removals That Constitute A Pattern

For there to be a change of placement based on a series of removals that constitute a pattern, all of the following three criteria must be met:
- Your child has been removed for more than 10 **cumulative** school days in the school year;
- The removals are for behavior substantially similar; **and**
- The removals are in close proximity to one another. (The other factors listed in the IDEA are length and total amount of time of the removals. However, they are not relevant considerations given California's suspension limitations.)

It is the administrator's responsibility to examine the above criteria and determine, on a case-by-case basis, whether there is a pattern of removals that constitute a change in placement. The best way to go about making this determination is for the administrator to consider the 10 cumulative days as a trigger to begin the analysis.

Once your child with special needs has reached 10 cumulative days of suspension in the school year, the administrator should review the previous suspensions that make up the 10 cumulative days and determine whether the behaviors are substantially similar. If the behaviors are not substantially similar, the analysis stops there, there is no change of placement based on a pattern, and a manifestation determination IEP is not required for your child.

However, if the administrator examines the previous suspensions and finds that the behaviors are substantially similar, the administrator must then examine the proximity of the removals to one another. If the removals were spread out over the course of 6 months, the criteria is not met and it is not a change of placement, and a manifestation determination IEP is not required. If the removals all occurred within the course of a 6-week period, the proximity criteria would be met, and the administrator should determine that there has been a change in placement based on a pattern of removals, and a manifestation determination IEP would be required for your child.

Manifestation Determination IEP

Once it has been determined that there is a proposed change in placement either because of an expulsion recommendation, 45 day removal, or a pattern of removals, a manifestation determination IEP must be held within 10 school days to determine whether the conduct is a manifestation of your child's disability.

The district, the parent, and relevant members of the IEP team must review all relevant information in the student's file: including your child's IEP, any teacher observations, and any relevant information provided by you. Once the above information has been reviewed, the IEP Team must discuss and answer the following questions:

- Whether the conduct in question was caused by, or had a direct and substantial relationship to, your child's disability; **or**
- Whether the conduct in question was the direct result of the District's failure to implement the IEP.

As these questions are being discussed by the IEP Team, it is important that the team clearly state the causal connection, or lack thereof, between the behavior and the disability or the specific elements of the IEP that were not implemented, if applicable, and how that failure lead to your child's behavior. If either question is answered in the affirmative, the behavior is a manifestation of the disability and the proposed change in placement cannot go forward.

If the IEP Team determines that the behavior **was** a manifestation of your child's disability, the team must:

- Conduct a functional behavioral assessment, and implement a behavioral support plan (BSP or PBIP), provided the District had not previously conducted such assessment;
- Review the BSP or PBIP if your child already has such a plan, and modify it, as necessary, to address the behavior; and
- Except in special circumstances, return your child to the placement from which s/he was removed, unless the you and the district agree to a change of placement as part of the modification of the BSP or PBIP.

If the team determines that the behavior **was not** a manifestation of your child's disability, then the proposed change in placement may proceed:

- General education discipline procedures apply.
- Your child may be suspended pending expulsion, if expulsion is being recommended.
- Services may be provided in an interim alternative educational setting.
- Your child should receive, as appropriate, a functional behavioral assessment, behavior intervention services and modifications, that are designed to address the behavior violation so that it does not recur

When there is a disciplinary change in placement following a determination that your child's behavior was not a manifestation of the disability or pursuant to a 45-day change in placement,

your child is entitled to services beginning the eleventh cumulative day of removal, as discussed in Services During Short Term Suspensions above. However, the services to be provided must be determined by the IEP Team.

IDEA Special Circumstances 45 - Day Placements

IDEA allows school personnel to remove your child with special needs to an interim alternative educational setting (IAES) for not more than 45 school days **without regard** to whether the behavior was a manifestation of your child's disability, when your child engages in the following conduct:

- Carries or possesses a weapon **to or at** school, **on** school premises, or **to or at** a school function;
- Knowingly possesses or uses illegal drugs, or sells or solicits the sale of a controlled substance, while **at** school, **on** school premises, or **at** a school function; or
- Inflicted serious bodily injury upon another person while **at** school, **on** school premises, **or** at a school function.

There are a few important things to note about this provision. First, the district's ability to utilize this provision for conduct that violates any of these sections is limited mostly to conduct that occurs at school or school functions. If the conduct involves a weapon, the district may also utilize this provision if the possession of the weapon occurs on the way to school. Practically speaking, the administrator must be able to establish that the conduct occurred within the applicable jurisdiction in order to remove your child with special needs to a 45-day interim placement for violation of any of these sections.

For example, if a fight that resulted in serious bodily injury occurred after school, off school grounds, the district would not be able to utilize the 45-day removal provision, as the conduct occurred outside of the jurisdiction for this section. The school could still suspend your child for the conduct pursuant to 48900(a)(1) & (2), and potentially recommend expulsion based on 48900(a)(1) & (2) and secondary findings, which are subject to the broader jurisdictional statement contained at 48900(s). However, if the IEP Team determined that the conduct was a manifestation of your child's disability, the expulsion process would stop and the student would be able to return to the placement from which s/he was removed.

Second, the 45-day removal provision is significant in that it is essentially sanctioned discrimination, as it allows your child with special needs who has engaged in one of the listed behaviors to be removed to an IAES for behavior that is a manifestation of her/his disability, **without your consent**. Using the same example above, let's say the fight and serious bodily injury occurred after school but on school grounds. The IEP team finds that the behavior is a manifestation of your child's disability, which would normally require that your child be returned to the placement from which s/he was removed. However, because the conduct occurred on campus, the 45-day removal provision can be utilized and your child can be placed in an IAES for up to 45 days, even though the behavior was a manifestation of her/his disability and the expulsion recommendation could not go forward.

Third, the basic assumptions that support using this process are: 1) the behavior is a manifestation of your child's disability, and 2) there is disagreement between you and the school about where your child should be placed following the conduct. Therefore, when utilizing the 45-day removal provision, it is important for the administrator to think about it as a time-out, an opportunity to have your child safely maintained in the IAES while the IEP Team explores alternative placement options that you can agree to. If it becomes apparent that the IEP Team cannot reach agreement about placement, the 45-day removal process allows the district and/or parents to pursue an administrative placement determination, while the student is still safely maintained in the IAES.

Lastly, because placement in the IAES is a change of placement, the location of the IAES and the services to be provided in the IAES must be determined by the IEP team. Additionally, your child should receive, as appropriate, a functional behavioral assessment, behavior intervention services, and modifications that are designed to address the behavior violation so that it does not recur.

10

Disciplinary Appeals

Procedures

If you disagree with the IEP team's manifestation determination or disciplinary change in placement, you have a right to file a disciplinary appeal.

Similarly, if the district believes that maintaining the current placement of your child is substantially likely to result in injury to your child or others, the district has the right to file a disciplinary appeal.

The appeals are filed with the Office of Administrative Hearings ("OAH") and are presided over by an Administrative Law Judge ("ALJ"). IDEA requires that the appeal be expedited, such that the hearing must occur within 20 school days of the date that the hearing is requested and the hearing decision must be rendered within 10 school days after the hearing has concluded. Your child remains in the IAES pending the decision of the ALJ or until the expiration of the 45-day placement, whichever occurs first, unless you and the district agree otherwise.

Authority of the Hearing Officer

The ALJ hearing the disciplinary appeal has only two options when rendering a decision. The ALJ may order the return of your child to the placement from which s/he was removed. This would mean that the ALJ found that the IEP Team's manifestation determination or placement decision was not appropriate or, if the appeal was filed by the district, that the district did not establish that it had done all it could to maintain your child safely in her/his original placement.

Alternatively, the ALJ may order a change of placement to the appropriate IAES for not more than 45 school days, if the ALJ determines that maintaining the current placement of your child is substantially likely to result in injury to your child or others. This would mean that the ALJ found that the determination of the IEP Team was appropriate or that your child could not be safely maintained in the original placement.

However, it is important to note that the authority of the ALJ to change your child's placement pursuant to a disciplinary appeal is limited to 45 days. Therefore, this is not a permanent solution to an IEP Team placement disagreement, because if the IEP Team cannot reach an agreement regarding placement prior to the expiration of the 45 days, your child has a right to return to the original placement from which s/he was removed.

11

Protections for Children Not Yet Eligible for Special Education

There is a group of general education students who have not been identified as eligible for special education, who engage in conduct violations that could potentially lead to a change in placement (i.e. expulsion recommendation), and who are entitled to the procedural safeguard provided by IDEA.

Whether or not a particular student is entitled to the IDEA procedural safeguards will depend on whether the district may be deemed to have knowledge that the student was, or may be, a student with a disability at the time the student engaged the conduct violation. The determination of whether the district may be deemed to have knowledge it typically made by the school site administrator.

Is the District Deemed to Have Knowledge?

Below are the three criteria for determining whether the district may be deemed to have knowledge. I will first explain the criteria, then provide examples of each situation, then summarize the implications of what it means for a district to be deemed to have knowledge.

One, the parent of the student has expressed concern in writing, to supervisory or administrative personnel of the appropriate educational agency or to a teacher of the student, that the student is in need of special education. In this scenario, if the parent sent a letter, email, etc., to the student's teacher or a school administrator indicating that the parent believes that the student may need special education services, prior to the student engaging in the conduct violation, the district would be deemed to have knowledge.

Two, the parent of the student has requested a special education evaluation. In this scenario, the parent came into the office and asked the clerk what the process is for her to have her child assessed for special education. The clerk described the process and asked the parent to make her request in writing to start the process. Two weeks have passed and the parent has not turned in her written request for an evaluation, but her daughter has engaged in a conduct violation during this time and is facing an expulsion recommendation. In this scenario, the district would be deemed to have knowledge.

Third, the teacher of the student, or other personnel of the district, has expressed specific concerns about a pattern of behavior demonstrated by the student, directly to the director of special education or to other supervisory personnel. In this scenario, the school is holding an SST meeting for the student. During the meeting the teacher expresses specific concerns about the student's behavior in his class that the SST team tries to address with modifications and supports. Shortly following the meeting, the student engages in a conduct violation and is facing an expulsion recommendation. In this scenario, the district would be deemed to have knowledge.

Once the school administrator has been informed that there may be a basis of knowledge, s/he would be expected to investigate the allegation and, if substantiated, determine that there is a basis of knowledge and proceed to the next steps.

When a Basis of Knowledge Exists

If there is a basis of knowledge that your child was, or may have been a student with a disability at the time s/he engaged in the conduct violation, then s/he is entitled to special education protections. Practically speaking, all this means is that the school will need to follow some additional procedural requirements before it can determine whether it has the authority to discipline your child.

Once a basis of knowledge has been established, the District must follow the steps below:

- Conduct an expedited comprehensive assessment (Ideally within 30 days);
- Hold an IEP to determine whether your child meets the IDEA eligibility criteria;
- If your child is not eligible for special education, the IDEA process stops, your child is a general education student, and general education discipline procedures apply;
- If your child is eligible for special education, the district must complete the development of the IEP and then conduct a manifestation determination based on the IEP just developed;
- If the behavior is found **to be a manifestation** of your child's disability, the general education disciplinary process stops and your child is placed in the FAPE placement identified in the newly developed IEP and a functional behavioral assessment should be conducted to address the behavior at issue;
- If the behavior is found **not to be a manifestation** of your child's disability, the general education discipline procedures apply and your child may be disciplined for the conduct violation, subject to receiving continued educational services in the alternative setting.

Exceptions To There Being A Basis of Knowledge

There are three situations in which the district will not be deemed to have knowledge, regardless of whether any of the scenarios above have occurred. They are:

- The parent has not allowed an evaluation of the child;
- The parent has refused services; or
- The child has been evaluated and determined not to be a child with a disability. (This evaluation should have occurred within the calendar year)

These exceptions recognize that situations exist where the student has been evaluated and the parents have not allowed the district to properly serve the student. In these instances, the student would not be entitled to the IDEA protections and would be treated as a general education student for disciplinary purposes.

When There is Not A Basis of Knowledge

If the administrator, following an investigation into the matter, is unable to substantiate the allegation that the district has a basis of knowledge, then your child is a general education student and general education disciplinary procedures apply. However, IDEA requires that if you make a request for an evaluation during the time period in which your child is subjected to disciplinary action, the evaluation must be conducted in an expedited manner. Pending the results of this evaluation, your child shall remain in the disciplinary educational placement determined by school authorities, and the outcome of the evaluation will not impact the previous discipline levied against your child.

Appendix

*Note: **Appendix D through M** are only sample forms. Every district creates its own forms and the forms in your district may or may not look like these samples. These samples are only meant to give you an example of the type of documentation you can expect throughout the discipline process.

2017 California Education Code Section 48900

State of California

EDUCATION CODE

Section 48900

48900. A pupil shall not be suspended from school or recommended for expulsion, unless the superintendent of the school district or the principal of the school in which the pupil is enrolled determines that the pupil has committed an act as defined pursuant to any of subdivisions (a) to (r), inclusive:
(a) (1) Caused, attempted to cause, or threatened to cause physical injury to another person.
(2) Willfully used force or violence upon the person of another, except in self-defense.
(b) Possessed, sold, or otherwise furnished a firearm, knife, explosive, or other dangerous object, unless, in the case of possession of an object of this type, the pupil had obtained written permission to possess the item from a certificated school employee, which is concurred in by the principal or the designee of the principal.
(c) Unlawfully possessed, used, sold, or otherwise furnished, or been under the influence of, a controlled substance listed in Chapter 2 (commencing with Section 11053) of Division 10 of the Health and Safety Code, an alcoholic beverage, or an intoxicant of any kind.
(d) Unlawfully offered, arranged, or negotiated to sell a controlled substance listed in Chapter 2 (commencing with Section 11053) of Division 10 of the Health and Safety Code, an alcoholic

beverage, or an intoxicant of any kind, and either sold, delivered, or otherwise furnished to a person another liquid, substance, or material and represented the liquid, substance, or material as a controlled substance, alcoholic beverage, or intoxicant.

(e) Committed or attempted to commit robbery or extortion.

(f) Caused or attempted to cause damage to school property or private property. (g) Stole or attempted to steal school property or private property.

(h) Possessed or used tobacco, or products containing tobacco or nicotine products, including, but not limited to, cigarettes, cigars, miniature cigars, clove cigarettes, smokeless tobacco, snuff, chew packets, and betel. However, this section does not prohibit the use or possession by a pupil of his or her own prescription products.

(i) Committed an obscene act or engaged in habitual profanity or vulgarity.

(j) Unlawfully possessed or unlawfully offered, arranged, or negotiated to sell drug paraphernalia, as defined in Section 11014.5 of the Health and Safety Code.

(k) (1) Disrupted school activities or otherwise willfully defied the valid authority of supervisors, teachers, administrators, school officials, or other school personnel engaged in the performance of their duties.

(2) Except as provided in Section 48910, a pupil enrolled in kindergarten or any of grades 1 to 3, inclusive, shall not be suspended for any of the acts enumerated in this subdivision, and this subdivision shall not constitute grounds for a pupil enrolled in kindergarten or any of grades 1 to 12, inclusive, to be recommended for expulsion. This paragraph shall become inoperative on July 1, 2018, unless a later enacted statute that becomes operative before July 1, 2018, deletes or extends that date.

(l) Knowingly received stolen school property or private property.

(m) Possessed an imitation firearm. As used in this section, "imitation firearm" means a replica of a firearm that is so substantially similar in physical properties to an existing firearm as to lead a reasonable person to conclude that the replica is a firearm.

(n) Committed or attempted to commit a sexual assault as defined in Section 261, 266c, 286, 288, 288a, or 289 of the Penal Code or committed a sexual battery as defined in Section 243.4 of the Penal Code.

(o) Harassed, threatened, or intimidated a pupil who is a complaining witness or a witness in a school disciplinary proceeding for purposes of either preventing that pupil from being a witness or retaliating against that pupil for being a witness, or both.

(p) Unlawfully offered, arranged to sell, negotiated to sell, or sold the prescription drug Soma.

(q) Engaged in, or attempted to engage in, hazing. For purposes of this subdivision, "hazing" means a method of initiation or preinitiation into a pupil organization or body, whether or not the organization or body is officially recognized by an educational institution, that is likely to cause serious bodily injury or personal degradation or disgrace resulting in physical or mental harm to a former, current, or prospective pupil. For purposes of this subdivision, "hazing" does not include athletic events or school-sanctioned events.

(r) Engaged in an act of bullying. For purposes of this subdivision, the following terms have the following meanings:

(1) "Bullying" means any severe or pervasive physical or verbal act or conduct, including communications made in writing or by means of an electronic act, and including one or more acts committed by a pupil or group of pupils as defined in Section 48900.2, 48900.3, or 48900.4, directed toward one or more pupils that has or can be reasonably predicted to have the effect of one or more of the following:

(A) Placing a reasonable pupil or pupils in fear of harm to that pupil's or those pupils' person or property.

(B) Causing a reasonable pupil to experience a substantially detrimental effect on his or her physical or mental health.

(C) Causing a reasonable pupil to experience substantial interference with his or her academic performance.

(D) Causing a reasonable pupil to experience substantial interference with his or her ability to participate in or benefit from the services, activities, or privileges provided by a school.

(2) (A) "Electronic act" means the creation or transmission originated on or off the schoolsite, by means of an electronic device, including, but not limited to, a telephone, wireless telephone, or other wireless communication device, computer, or pager, of a communication, including, but not limited to, any of the following:

(i) A message, text, sound, video, or image.

(ii) A post on a social network Internet Web site, including, but not limited to:

(I) Posting to or creating a burn page. "Burn page" means an Internet Web site created for the purpose of having one or more of the effects listed in paragraph (1).

(II) Creating a credible impersonation of another actual pupil for the purpose of having one or more of the effects listed in paragraph (1). "Credible impersonation" means to knowingly and without consent impersonate a pupil for the purpose of bullying the pupil and such that another pupil would reasonably believe, or has reasonably believed, that the pupil was or is the pupil who was impersonated.

(III) Creating a false profile for the purpose of having one or more of the effects listed in paragraph (1). "False profile" means a profile of a fictitious pupil or a profile using the likeness or attributes of an actual pupil other than the pupil who created the false profile.

(iii) An act of cyber sexual bullying.

(I) For purposes of this clause, "cyber sexual bullying" means the dissemination of, or the solicitation or incitement to disseminate, a photograph or other visual recording by a pupil to another pupil or to school personnel by means of an electronic act that has or can be reasonably predicted to have one or more of the effects described in subparagraphs (A) to (D), inclusive, of paragraph (1). A photograph or other visual recording, as described above, shall include the depiction of a nude, semi-nude, or sexually explicit photograph or other visual recording of a minor where the minor is identifiable from the photograph, visual recording, or other electronic act.

(II) For purposes of this clause, "cyber sexual bullying" does not include a depiction, portrayal, or image that has any serious literary, artistic, educational, political, or scientific value or that involves athletic events or school-sanctioned activities.

(B) Notwithstanding paragraph (1) and subparagraph (A), an electronic act shall not constitute pervasive conduct solely on the basis that it has been transmitted on the Internet or is currently posted on the Internet.

(3) "Reasonable pupil" means a pupil, including, but not limited to, an exceptional needs pupil, who exercises average care, skill, and judgment in conduct for a person of his or her age, or for a person of his or her age with his or her exceptional needs.

(s) A pupil shall not be suspended or expelled for any of the acts enumerated in this section unless the act is related to a school activity or school attendance occurring within a school under the jurisdiction of the superintendent of the school district or principal or occurring within any other school district. A pupil may be suspended or expelled for acts that are enumerated in this section and related to a school activity or school attendance that occur at any time, including, but not limited to, any of the following:

(1) While on school grounds.
(2) While going to or coming from school.
(3) During the lunch period whether on or off the campus.
(4) During, or while going to or coming from, a school-sponsored activity.

(t) A pupil who aids or abets, as defined in Section 31 of the Penal Code, the infliction or attempted infliction of physical injury to another person may be subject to suspension, but not expulsion, pursuant to this section, except that a pupil who has been adjudged by a juvenile court to have committed, as an aider and abettor, a crime of physical violence in which the victim suffered great bodily injury or serious bodily injury shall be subject to discipline pursuant to subdivision (a).

(u) As used in this section, "school property" includes, but is not limited to, electronic files and databases.

(v) For a pupil subject to discipline under this section, a superintendent of the school district or principal may use his or her discretion to provide alternatives to suspension or expulsion that are age appropriate and designed to address and correct the pupil's specific misbehavior as specified in Section 48900.5.

(w) It is the intent of the Legislature that alternatives to suspension or expulsion be imposed against a pupil who is truant, tardy, or otherwise absent from school activities.

(Amended by Stats. 2016, Ch. 419, Sec. 2.5. (AB 2536) Effective January 1, 2017.)

2017 California Education Code Section 48900.5

State of California

EDUCATION CODE

Section 48900.5

48900.5. (a) Suspension, including supervised suspension as described in Section 48911.1, shall be imposed only when other means of correction fail to bring about proper conduct. A school district may document the other means of correction used and place that documentation in the pupil's record, which may be accessed pursuant to Section 49069. However, a pupil, including an individual with exceptional needs, as defined in Section 56026, may be suspended, subject to Section 1415 of Title 20 of the United States Code, for any of the reasons enumerated in Section 48900 upon a first offense, if the principal or superintendent of schools determines that the pupil violated subdivision (a), (b), (c), (d), or (e) of Section 48900 or that the pupil's presence causes a danger to persons.
(b) Other means of correction include, but are not limited to, the following:
(1) A conference between school personnel, the pupil's parent or guardian, and the pupil.
(2) Referrals to the school counselor, psychologist, social worker, child welfare attendance personnel, or other school support service personnel for case management and counseling.
(3) Study teams, guidance teams, resource panel teams, or other intervention-related teams that assess the behavior, and develop and implement individualized plans to address the behavior in partnership with the pupil and his or her parents.

(4) Referral for a comprehensive psychosocial or psychoeducational assessment, including for purposes of creating an individualized education program, or a plan adopted pursuant to Section 504 of the federal Rehabilitation Act of 1973 (29 U.S.C. Sec. 794(a)).

(5) Enrollment in a program for teaching prosocial behavior or anger management.

(6) Participation in a restorative justice program.

(7) A positive behavior support approach with tiered interventions that occur during the school day on campus.

(8) After-school programs that address specific behavioral issues or expose pupils to positive activities and behaviors, including, but not limited to, those operated in collaboration with local parent and community groups.

(9) Any of the alternatives described in Section 48900.6.

(Amended by Stats. 2012, Ch. 425, Sec. 3. (AB 1729) Effective January 1, 2013.)

2017 California Education Code Section 48915

State of California

EDUCATION CODE

Section 48915

48915. (a) (1) Except as provided in subdivisions (c) and (e), the principal or the superintendent of schools shall recommend the expulsion of a pupil for any of the following acts committed at school or at a school activity off school grounds, unless the principal or superintendent determines that expulsion should not be recommended under the circumstances or that an alternative means of correction would address the conduct:

(A) Causing serious physical injury to another person, except in self-defense.

(B) Possession of any knife or other dangerous object of no reasonable use to the pupil.

(C) Unlawful possession of any controlled substance listed in Chapter 2(commencing with Section 11053) of Division 10 of the Health and Safety Code,except for either of the following:

(i) The first offense for the possession of not more than one avoirdupois ounce of marijuana, other than concentrated cannabis.

(ii) The possession of over-the-counter medication for use by the pupil for medical purposes or medication prescribed for the pupil by a physician.

(D) Robbery or extortion.

(E) Assault or battery, as defined in Sections 240 and 242 of the Penal Code, upon any school employee.

(2) If the principal or the superintendent of schools makes a determination as described in paragraph (1), he or she is encouraged to do so as quickly as possible to ensure that the pupil does not lose instructional time.

(b) Upon recommendation by the principal or the superintendent of schools, or by a hearing officer or administrative panel appointed pursuant to subdivision (d) ofSection 48918, the governing board of a school district may order a pupil expelled upon finding that the pupil committed an act listed in paragraph (1) of subdivision(a) or in subdivision (a), (b), (c), (d), or (e) of Section 48900. A decision to expel a pupil for any of those acts shall be based on a finding of one or both of the following:

(1) Other means of correction are not feasible or have repeatedly failed to bring about proper conduct.

(2) Due to the nature of the act, the presence of the pupil causes a continuing danger to the physical safety of the pupil or others.

(c) The principal or superintendent of schools shall immediately suspend, pursuant to Section 48911, and shall recommend expulsion of a pupil that he or she determines has committed any of the following acts at school or at a school activity off school grounds:

(1) Possessing, selling, or otherwise furnishing a firearm. This subdivision does not apply to an act of possessing a firearm if the pupil had obtained prior written permission to possess the firearm from a certificated school employee, which is concurred in by the principal or the designee of the principal. This subdivision applies to an act of possessing a firearm only if the possession is verified by an employee of a school district. The act of possessing an imitation firearm, as defined in subdivision(m) of Section 48900, is not an offense for which suspension or expulsion is mandatory pursuant to this subdivision and subdivision (d), but it is an offense for which suspension, or expulsion pursuant to subdivision (e), may be imposed.

(2) Brandishing a knife at another person.

(3) Unlawfully selling a controlled substance listed in Chapter 2 (commencing with Section 11053) of Division 10 of the Health and Safety Code.

(4) Committing or attempting to commit a sexual assault as defined in subdivision(n) of Section 48900 or committing a sexual battery as defined in subdivision (n) of Section 48900.

(5) Possession of an explosive.

(d) The governing board of a school district shall order a pupil expelled upon finding that the pupil committed an act listed in subdivision (c), and shall refer that pupil to a program of study that meets all of the following conditions:

(1) Is appropriately prepared to accommodate pupils who exhibit discipline problems.

(2) Is not provided at a comprehensive middle, junior, or senior high school, or at any elementary school.

(3) Is not housed at the school site attended by the pupil at the time of suspension.

(e) Upon recommendation by the principal or the superintendent of schools, or by a hearing officer or administrative panel appointed pursuant to subdivision (d) ofSection 48918, the governing board of a school district may order a pupil expelled upon finding that the pupil, at school or at a school activity off of school grounds violated subdivision (f), (g), (h), (i), (j), (k), (l), or (m) of Section 48900, or Section 48900.2, 48900.3, or 48900.4, and either of the following:

(1) That other means of correction are not feasible or have repeatedly failed to bring about proper conduct.

(2) That due to the nature of the violation, the presence of the pupil causes a continuing danger to the physical safety of the pupil or others.

(f) The governing board of a school district shall refer a pupil who has been expelled pursuant to subdivision (b) or (e) to a program of study that meets all of the conditions specified in subdivision (d). Notwithstanding this subdivision, with respect to a pupil expelled pursuant to subdivision (e), if the county superintendent of schools certifies that an alternative program of study is not available at a site away from a comprehensive middle, junior, or senior high school, or an elementary school, and that the only option for placement is at another comprehensive middle, junior, or senior high school, or another elementary school, the pupil may be referred to a program of study that is provided at a comprehensive middle, junior, or senior high school, or at an elementary school.

(g) As used in this section, "knife" means any dirk, dagger, or other weapon with a fixed, sharpened blade fitted primarily for stabbing, a weapon with a blade fitted primarily for stabbing, a weapon with a blade longer than 3 1/2 inches, a folding knife with a blade that locks into place, or a razor with an unguarded blade.

(h) As used in this section, the term "explosive" means "destructive device" as described in Section 921 of Title 18 of the United States Code.

(Amended by Stats. 2012, Ch. 431, Sec. 3. (AB 2537) Effective January 1, 2013.)

Glossary of Discipline Definitions

"Hearsay"

A statement made out of court that is offered in court, by someone other than the declarant, as evidence to prove the truth of the matter asserted – secondhand information.

"Direct Evidence"

Evidence offered by someone with firsthand knowledge of the event.

"Percipient Witness"

A witness who has firsthand knowledge of the event. *A subpoena can only be issued to compel the personal appearance of a percipient witness.

"Firearm"
Any device, designed to be used as a weapon, from which is expelled through a barrel a projectile by the force of any explosion or other form of combustion.
Penal Code sec. 12001(b).

"Self-Defense"
Free from fault (no provocation), no convenient mode of escape by retreat or declining the combat, and present impending peril creating a reasonable belief of necessity.

"Serious physical injury" - 48915 (a) (1) definition

Serious physical impairments of physical condition, such as loss of consciousness, concussion, bone fracture, protracted loss or impairment of function of any bodily member or organ, a wound requiring suturing, and serious disfigurement. [Title 5, Section 11993(q).]

Special Education Discipline Definitions

"Dangerous Weapon"

The IDEA allows districts to remove a student to an interim alternative educational setting for up to 45 school days for carrying or possessing a weapon. According to both IDEA '97 and IDEA '04, the term "'weapon' has the meaning given the term '**dangerous weapon**' under Section 930(g)(2) of Title 18, United States Code."

The section, in turn, states: "The term '**dangerous weapon**' means a weapon, device, instrument, material, or substance, animate or inanimate, that is used for, or is readily capable of, causing death or serious bodily injury, except that such term does not include a pocket knife with a blade of less than 2 1/2 inches in length.

"Serious Bodily Injury" (Special education 45-day placement definition)
– means bodily injury that involves-

    (A) a substantial risk of death;

    (B) extreme physical pain;

    (C) protracted and obvious disfigurement; or

    (D) protracted loss or impairment of the function of a bodily member, organ, or mental faculty

    18 U.S.C. § 1365(h)(3)

"Change of Placement" (special education)
1) More than 10 consecutive school days; or
2) Pattern
   Total more than 10 school days in the school year;
   Behavior substantially similar; **and**
   Additional factors, length, total amount of time, proximity of removals to each other.
(Determined by the District on case-by-case basis)

Student Statement Form

School Name _____ Date: _____ Student #:_____

SWORN DECLARATION OF

Print student name

I, _____ , declare the following:

_____
_____
_____
_____
_____
_____
_____
_____
_____
_____
_____
_____

I have read this declaration and do declare under penalty of perjury and the laws of the State of California that it is true and correct to the best of my knowledge.

Dated: _____

Signature

Sworn Declaration of Witness

SWORN DECLARATION OF WITNESS
Education Code Section 48918, Subsection (f)
(Unreasonable risk of harm)

In matter of the suspension and possible expulsion of _____

a student enrolled at _____ school. I, _____,

feel the disclosure of my identity as a witness and my testimony as a witness at the hearing

would subject me to unreasonable risk of psychological or physical harm.

NARRATIVE: (Explain the unreasonable risk of psychological or physical harm)

_____
_____
_____
_____
_____
_____
_____

I declare under penalty of perjury that the foregoing is true and correct this

day _____ month _____, year _____

Declarant Signature: _____

Notice of Suspension

{Sample Included on Next Page}

********* School District
(School address)

Notification of Administrative Suspension from School

Date	School		Student's Phone Number		
Student's Name:	Last	First	Grade	Student ID	Birthdate
Suspension From: Day	Time	Date / /	Suspension Code:	Special Ed Student ☐ Yes ☐ No	
Day Return:	Time	Date / /	**Police Report** ☐ N/A ☐ Pending ☐ Filed #	**Expulsion Review** ☐ N/A ☐ Recommended ☐ Pending	

EDUCATION CODE SECTION 48900

- ☐ a.1. Caused, attempted to cause, or threatened to cause physical injury.
- ☐ a.2. Willfully used force or violence on another person, except in self defense.
- ☐ b. Possessed, sold or otherwise furnished any firearm, knife, explosive, or other dangerous object. ++
- ☐ c. Possessed, used, sold, furnished, or been under the influence of any controlled substance, alcohol, or intoxicant. ++
- ☐ d. Offered, arranged, or negotiated to sell a controlled substance, alcohol or intoxicant and then provided a replica substance. ++
- ☐ e. Attempted or committed robbery or extortion.
- ☐ f. Attempted or caused damage to school or private property.
- ☐ g. Attempted or stole school or private property.
- ☐ h. Possessed, or used a tobacco product.
- ☐ i. Committed an obscene act or engaged in habitual profanity or vulgarity.
- ☐ j. Possessed, offered, arranged, or negotiated to sell drug paraphernalia.
- ☐ k. Disrupted school activities or defied school personnel.
- ☐ l. Knowingly received stolen school or private property.
- ☐ m. Possessed an imitation firearm.++ - **if fires metallic projectile**
- ☐ n. Attempted or committed sexual assault or committed a sexual battery. ++
- ☐ o. Harassed, threatened, or intimidated a student complainant or witness in a school disciplinary matter.
- ☐ p. Unlawfully offered, arranged to sell, negotiated to sell, or sold the prescription drug Soma. ++
- ☐ q. Engaged in, or attempted to engage in, hazing.
- ☐ r. Engaged in an act of bullying, including electronic means ☐ 48900.2 ☐ 48900.3 ☐ 48900.4 (indicate which was violated)
- ☐ t. A pupil who aids or abets in the attempted or infliction of physical injury to another.
- ☐ .2 Committed sexual harassment. (Gr.4-12)
- ☐ .3 Attempted, threatened, caused, or participated in hate violence. (Grades 4-12)
- ☐ .4 Created an intimidating or hostile educational environment. (Gr.4-12)
- ☐ .7 Made terroristic threats against school officials or property.

++ **Indicates law enforcement MUST be notified**

MANDATORY RECOMMENDATION FOR EXPULSION
(Education Code 48915(c)):

- ☐ c. 1. Sale, possession or furnishing a firearm. ++
- ☐ c. 2. Brandishing a knife at another person. ++
- ☐ c. 3. Selling a controlled substance. ++
- ☐ c. 4. Sexual assault or sexual battery. ++
- ☐ c. 5. Possession of an explosive. ++

DISCRETIONARY MANDATORY RECOMMENDATION FOR EXPULSION
(Education Code 48915 (a)(1):

- ☐ 1.A Causing serious injury to another person, except in self-defense.++
- ☐ 1.B Possession of a knife, or other dangerous object of no reasonable use to the pupil.++
- ☐ 1.C Unlawful possession of any controlled substance except for the first offense for the possession of not more than one avoirdupois ounce of marijuana, other than concentrated cannabis, over the counter medications, or prescribed medication.++
- ☐ 1.D Robbery or extortion.
- ☐ 1.E Assault or battery on any school employee.++

Parent Conference   ☐ Held   ☐ Requested   ☐ Via Phone
Date:_____ Time:_____
Contact Name:_____

Student Conference ☐ Held ☐ Postponed until _____
Date:_____ Time:_____

Total Days Suspended in the School Year: _____

Factual explanation of incident(s): Date:_____ Time:_____
Location: ☐ On Campus ☐ Off Campus ☐ School activity off school grounds ☐ Attendance related
_____

Dear Parents/Guardians:

This suspension is in compliance with Education Code Section 48900 and 48915 et seq. The suspension has been discussed with your student and he/she has been given an opportunity to explain his/her side of the incident.* If a conference has been requested, please make every effort to attend. Under state law, you are required to respond to this request without delay. If you wish, you and your student may review his/her record as provided in Education Code 49069. Make-up work and/or tests may be provided for your student, if requested, for the period of suspension.

If you feel the suspension is inappropriate and have discussed your concerns with the school principal, you may appeal the suspension to (Name of appropriate person), Assistant Superintendent. Call the Educational Services Department, (***-****) for an appointment.
PLEASE NOTE: During the school day, your student must not be on or near any school campus. Supervision is the responsibility of the parent/guardian during the suspension.

By:_____
    Principal/Designee

*The principal or designee may suspend a student without a conference if an emergency situation exists.
State laws allow the principal to recommend suspension for violations of Education Code section 48900 subdivisions (a), (b), (c), (d), (e), and other subdivisions upon a first offense, if the pupil's presence is deemed to be a danger to persons.

© 2015 The Law Office of Dora J. Dome

Letter Extending Suspension Pending Expulsion

[DISTRICT LETTERHEAD]

LETTER EXTENDING SUSPENSION
PENDING EXPULSION

[Date]

[Address]

Re: [Student's Name]
     [Student's Birth Date]

Dear _____:

    The principal of [School Name] has recommended the expulsion of your [son/daughter/grandson/granddaughter], [Student's Name]. The Education Code sections on student suspension and expulsion were explained to you and [Student] during a meeting held in [Teacher/Administrator's Name] office on [Date]. The expulsion process follows the law as outlined by the Education Code.

    The incident of [Date], described in the attached Notice, demonstrates a clear breach of discipline and defiance of school rules and regulations by [Student's Name]. Therefore, I am extending the suspension until a decision on expulsion is reached by the Board of Education.

    I have determined that [Student's] presence at school would [cause a danger to persons or property and/or cause disruption of the instructional process]; therefore, [Student] is to remain away from school at all times during this suspension period. Arrangements for obtaining classwork to be completed at home may be made with [Student's] counselor or school administrator. Supervision of the pupil during the suspension is the responsibility of the parent or guardian.

It is important that you and [Student] meet with [Teacher or Administrator] as soon as possible to discuss the Statement of Charges and the hearing process. Please call [Enter phone number] to make an appointment.

Sincerely,

[Signature]
[Title]

cc:

Letter Extending Suspension Pending Expulsion - IDEA

[Date]

[Address]

        Re: [Student's Name]
                [Student's Birth Date]

Dear _____:

    The principal of [School Name] has recommended the expulsion of your [son/daughter/grandson/granddaughter], [Student's Name]. [Student] is a student with a disability pursuant to the IDEA. Therefore, before expulsion proceedings can be considered, [Student] is entitled to have an IEP team meeting within ten (10) school days of the date of suspension to determine whether there is a relationship between the reported misconduct and [Student's] disability.

    The Education Code sections on student suspension and expulsion were explained to you and [Student] during a meeting held in [Teacher/Administrator's Name] office on [Date]. The expulsion process follows the law as outlined by the Education Code.

    The incident of [Date] demonstrates a clear breach of discipline and defiance of school rules and regulations by [Student's Name]. Therefore, I am extending the suspension pending expulsion and until the IEP team has determined whether there is a relationship between the misconduct and [Student's] disability. If the IEP team determines that there is not a relationship between the conduct and [Student's] disability, the suspension will continue until a decision on expulsion is reached by the Board of Education.

I have determined that [Student's] presence at school would [cause a danger to persons or property and/or cause disruption of the instructional process]; therefore, [Student] is to remain away from school at all times during this suspension period. Beginning on the eleventh day of removal in a school year, [Student's] IEP will be implemented to the extent necessary to enable [him/her] to appropriately progress toward achieving the goals set out in [Student's] IEP, as determined by the IEP team.

Sincerely,

[Signature]
[Title]

Letter Terminating Expulsion Recommendation - IDEA

[Date]

[Address]

        Re: [Student's Name]
                    [Student's Birth Date]

Dear _____:

      The IEP team met on [Date] and determined that there was a relationship between the reported misconduct and [Student's] disability. Therefore, all disciplinary action will be terminated and [Student] will be returned to his/her previous placement.

                                      Sincerely,

                                      [Signature]
                                      [Title]

Expulsion Packet Checklist

____ Notice of Suspension Form

____ Principal Summary/Recommendation For Expulsion

____ Letter Extending Suspension Pending Expulsion

____ Notice of Hearing and Charges Letter

____ Incident Report(s)/ Witness Statements (Staff and students) (Redacted)

____ Evidence (Photos, weapon, police reports, medical records, etc)

____ Interventions AND Discipline History

____ Student Status reports

____ Grade Reports/ Transcripts/Attendance

____ Request for Continuance, if applicable

Expulsion Packet Table of Contents

INDEX OF ATTACHMENTS INCLUDED IN

THE RECOMMENDATION FOR EXPULSION OF

STUDENT NAME

CASE NO.

BEFORE THE [BOARD OF EDUCATION or ADMINISTRATIVE HEARING PANEL]

DATE

Document Title	Page
Suspension Letter & Notice of Suspension	
Principal's Recommendation For Expulsion	
Director's Notice of Meeting to Consider Extension of Suspension Letter	
Director's Notice of Extension of Suspension	
Notification of Recommendation for Expulsion and Expulsion Hearing	
Student Declaration	
Victim/Witness Statements	
Photograph of Item in Student's Possession	
Student Discipline Report: Referrals/Suspensions	
School Attendance Record & Truancy Documentation	
Remediation & Support Services Provided Student	
Teachers' Progress Reports	
Transcript Of Student's Grades	
Board Policy	**Appendix**
Copy Of Education Code 48900 & 48915 (Student Services)	
Copy Of School Rules & District Discipline Policy (Student Services)	

Stipulation and Request for Waiver

Stipulation and Request for Waiver of Expulsion Hearing
with Recommendation for Expulsion

To: ********, Superintendent
********** Unified School District

Re: Name of Student
School
Principal Recommending Expulsion

[Student Name Full], student, and [Parent Name], parent of student, acknowledge meeting with [Special Education Director or designee] on [meeting date]. We have been informed of and understand the right to due process with regard to the expulsion recommendation against [name of student] by [name of principal], of the ******** Unified School District.

Moreover, we received a copy of the Notice of Expulsion and Charges dated [Charge ltr date] and understand the contents of that notice.

We understand that the expulsion hearing has been scheduled for [Day/Date of Hearing], at [Time], in the [Name of District Office], located at [Address of District Office], California. In particular, we have been informed and understand that we have the right to a full evidentiary hearing, the right to appear in person or employ and be represented by counsel at this hearing, the right to inspect and obtain copies of all documents to be used at the hearing, the right to confront and question all witnesses who testify at the hearing, the right to question all evidence presented, and to present oral and documentary evidence on [student's name]'s behalf, including witnesses. We have received a written copy of these rights. We have also received a written description of the charges that led to the recommendation for expulsion, copies of applicable provisions of the California Education Code and District Rules and Regulations governing expulsions.

We stipulate and agree that [name of student] is subject to expulsion from the District for having committed acts in violation of Education Code section _____ [description of statutory offense]. [If required by Education Code section 48915] We further stipulate that other means of correction are not feasible or have repeatedly failed to bring about proper conduct or that due to the nature of the violation, the presence of the pupil causes a continuing danger to the physical safety of the pupil or others.

After careful consideration, we voluntarily request a waiver of the expulsion hearing before the ******** Unified School District Hearing Panel, located at [address]. We understand that the purpose and function of the waived hearing would have been for fact-finding and to submit recommendations to the Board of Education when the Board meets to deliberate and act on this matter. In addition to waiving the expulsion hearing, we also request that all legal time lines in this matter be waived.

We understand that an expulsion recommendation will be submitted to the Board of Education for its review and final action. The District administration will recommend that [student's name] be expelled for [one/two semester(s)], through [date].

We understand that the Board of Education will ensure that an education program is provided to [student's name] for the period of the expulsion. In addition we understand that the Board of Education will recommend a plan of rehabilitation for [student's name]. This rehabilitation plan may include, but not be limited to, periodic review as well as assessment at the time of review for readmission. The plan may also include recommendations for improved academic performance, tutoring, special education assessments, job training, counseling, employment, community service, or other rehabilitative programs.

We understand that at the conclusion of [student's name] expulsion term, [he/she] shall be reviewed for readmission to a school maintained by the District or to the school [student's name] last attended. Upon completion of the readmission process, the Board of Education will readmit [name of student], unless the Board of Education makes a finding that the pupil has not met the conditions of [his/her] rehabilitation plan or continues to pose a danger to campus safety or to other pupils or employees of the District.

By requesting this Waiver of Hearing on Expulsion, we acknowledge that, should the Board of Education vote not to accept the administration's recommendation, we retain the right to withdraw this Waiver of Expulsion Hearing and have the matter heard by the ******** Unified School District Hearing Panel

EXPULSION REHABILITATION PLAN:

[ADD TERMS OF REHAB PLAN]

[Name of Student]   Date

[Parent]   Date

[Parent]   Date

Special Education Discipline Regulations - 34 CFR 300.530 – 537

App n1 CFR 300.530 Authority of school personnel
App n2 CFR 300.531 Determination of setting
App n3 CFR 300.532 Appeal
App n4 CFR 300.533 Placement during appeals
App n5 CFR 300.534 Protections for children not determined eligible for special education
App n6 CFR 300.535 Referral to and action by law enforcement and judicial authorities
App n7 CFR 300.536 Change of placement because of disciplinary removals
App n8 CFR 300.537 State enforcement mechanisms

n1 Authority of School Personnel

Code of Federal Regulations
 Title 34. Education
  Subtitle B. Regulations of the Offices of the Department of Education
   Chapter III. Office of Special Education and Rehabilitative Services, Department of Education
    Part 300. Assistance to States for the Education of Children with Disabilities (Refs & Annos)
     Subpart E. Procedural Safeguards
      Discipline Procedures

34 C.F.R. § 300.530
§ 300.530 Authority of school personnel.
Effective: October 13, 2006
Currentness

(a) Case-by-case determination. School personnel may consider any unique circumstances on a case-by-case basis when determining whether a change in placement, consistent with the other requirements of this section, is appropriate for a child with a disability who violates a code of student conduct.

(b) General.

(1) School personnel under this section may remove a child with a disability who violates a code of student conduct from his or her current placement to an appropriate interim alternative educational setting, another setting, or suspension, for not more than 10 consecutive school days (to the extent those alternatives are applied to children without disabilities), and for additional removals of not more than 10 consecutive school days in that same school year for separate incidents of misconduct (as long as those removals do not constitute a change of placement under § 300.536).

(2) After a child with a disability has been removed from his or her current placement for 10 school days in the same school year, during any subsequent days of removal the public agency must provide services to the extent required under paragraph (d) of this section.

(c) Additional authority. For disciplinary changes in placement that would exceed 10 consecutive school days, if the behavior that gave rise to the violation of the school code is determined not to be a manifestation of the child's disability pursuant to paragraph (e) of this section, school personnel may apply the relevant disciplinary procedures to children with disabilities in the same manner and for the same duration as the procedures would be applied to children without disabilities, except as provided in paragraph (d) of this section.

(d) Services.

(1) A child with a disability who is removed from the child's current placement pursuant to paragraphs (c), or (g) of this section must—

(i) Continue to receive educational services, as provided in § 300.101(a), so as to enable the child to continue to participate in the general education curriculum, although in another setting, and to progress toward meeting the goals set out in the child's IEP; and

(ii) Receive, as appropriate, a functional behavioral assessment, and behavioral intervention services and modifications, that are designed to address the behavior violation so that it does not recur.

(2) The services required by paragraph (d)(1), (d)(3), (d)(4), and (d)(5) of this section may be provided in an interim alternative educational setting.

(3) A public agency is only required to provide services during periods of removal to a child with a disability who has been removed from his or her current placement for 10 school days or less in that school year, if it provides services to a child without disabilities who is similarly removed.

(4) After a child with a disability has been removed from his or her current placement for 10 school days in the same school year, if the current removal is for not more than 10 consecutive school days and is not a change of placement under § 300.536, school personnel, in consultation with at least one of the child's teachers, determine the extent to which services are needed, as provided in § 300.101(a), so as to enable the child to continue to participate in the general education curriculum, although in another setting, and to progress toward meeting the goals set out in the child's IEP.

(5) If the removal is a change of placement under § 300.536, the child's IEP Team determines appropriate services under paragraph (d)(1) of this section.

(e) Manifestation determination.

(1) Within 10 school days of any decision to change the placement of a child with a disability because of a violation of a code of student conduct, the LEA, the parent, and relevant

members of the child's IEP Team (as determined by the parent and the LEA) must review all relevant information in the student's file, including the child's IEP, any teacher observations, and any relevant information provided by the parents to determine—

(i) If the conduct in question was caused by, or had a direct and substantial relationship to, the child's disability; or

(ii) If the conduct in question was the direct result of the LEA's failure to implement the IEP.

(2) The conduct must be determined to be a manifestation of the child's disability if the LEA, the parent, and relevant members of the child's IEP Team determine that a condition in either paragraph (e)(1)(i) or (1)(ii) of this section was met.

(3) If the LEA, the parent, and relevant members of the child's IEP Team determine the condition described in paragraph (e)(1)(ii) of this section was met, the LEA must take immediate steps to remedy those deficiencies.

(f) Determination that behavior was a manifestation. If the LEA, the parent, and relevant members of the IEP Team make the determination that the conduct was a manifestation of the child's disability, the IEP Team must—

(1) Either—

(i) Conduct a functional behavioral assessment, unless the LEA had conducted a functional behavioral assessment before the behavior that resulted in the change of placement occurred, and implement a behavioral intervention plan for the child; or

(ii) If a behavioral intervention plan already has been developed, review the behavioral intervention plan, and modify it, as necessary, to address the behavior; and

(2) Except as provided in paragraph (g) of this section, return the child to the placement from which the child was removed, unless the parent and the LEA agree to a change of placement as part of the modification of the behavioral intervention plan.

(g) Special circumstances. School personnel may remove a student to an interim alternative educational setting for not more than 45 school days without regard to whether the behavior is determined to be a manifestation of the child's disability, if the child—

(1) Carries a weapon to or possesses a weapon at school, on school premises, or to or at a school function under the jurisdiction of an SEA or an LEA;

(2) Knowingly possesses or uses illegal drugs, or sells or solicits the sale of a controlled substance, while at school, on school premises, or at a school function under the jurisdiction of an SEA or an LEA; or

(3) Has inflicted serious bodily injury upon another person while at school, on school premises, or at a school function under the jurisdiction of an SEA or an LEA.

(h) Notification. On the date on which the decision is made to make a removal that constitutes a change of placement of a child with a disability because of a violation of a code of student conduct, the LEA must notify the parents of that decision, and provide the parents the procedural safeguards notice described in § 300.504.

(i) Definitions. For purposes of this section, the following definitions apply:

(1) Controlled substance means a drug or other substance identified under schedules I, II, III, IV, or V in section 202(c) of the Controlled Substances Act (21 U.S.C. 812(c)).

(2) Illegal drug means a controlled substance; but does not include a controlled substance that is legally possessed or used under the supervision of a licensed health-care professional or that is legally possessed or used under any other authority under that Act or under any other provision of Federal law.

(3) Serious bodily injury has the meaning given the term "serious bodily injury" under paragraph (3) of subsection (h) of section 1365 of title 18, United States Code.

(4) Weapon has the meaning given the term "dangerous weapon" under paragraph (2) of the first subsection (g) of section 930 of title 18, United States Code.

(Authority: 20 U.S.C. 1415(k)(1) and (7))

SOURCE: 71 FR 46755, Aug. 14, 2006; 72 FR 17781, April 9, 2007; 80 FR 23666, April 28, 2015, unless otherwise noted.

AUTHORITY: 20 U.S.C. 1221e–3, 1406, 1411–1419, 3474, unless otherwise noted.

Notes of Decisions (13)
Current through March 24, 2016; 81 FR 16051.

| End of Document | © 2016 Thomson Reuters. No claim to original U.S. Government Works. |

n2 Determination of Setting

Code of Federal Regulations
  Title 34. Education
    Subtitle B. Regulations of the Offices of the Department of Education
      Chapter III. Office of Special Education and Rehabilitative Services, Department of Education
        Part 300. Assistance to States for the Education of Children with Disabilities (Refs & Annos)
          Subpart E. Procedural Safeguards
            Discipline Procedures

34 C.F.R. § 300.531
§ 300.531 Determination of setting.
Effective: October 13, 2006

Currentness

The child's IEP Team determines the interim alternative educational setting for services under § 300.530(c), (d)(5), and (g).

(Authority: 20 U.S.C. 1415(k)(2))

SOURCE: 71 FR 46755, Aug. 14, 2006; 72 FR 17781, April 9, 2007; 80 FR 23666, April 28, 2015, unless otherwise noted.

AUTHORITY: 20 U.S.C. 1221e–3, 1406, 1411–1419, 3474, unless otherwise noted.

Notes of Decisions (1)

Current through March 24, 2016; 81 FR 16051.

| End of Document | © 2016 Thomson Reuters. No claim to original U.S. Government Works. |

n3 Appeal

Code of Federal Regulations
  Title 34. Education
    Subtitle B. Regulations of the Offices of the Department of Education
      Chapter III. Office of Special Education and Rehabilitative Services, Department of Education
        Part 300. Assistance to States for the Education of Children with Disabilities (Refs & Annos)
          Subpart E. Procedural Safeguards
            Discipline Procedures

34 C.F.R. § 300.532

§ 300.532 Appeal.

Effective: October 13, 2006

Currentness

(a) General. The parent of a child with a disability who disagrees with any decision regarding placement under §§ 300.530 and 300.531, or the manifestation determination under § 300.530(e), or an LEA that believes that maintaining the current placement of the child is substantially likely to result in injury to the child or others, may appeal the decision by requesting a hearing. The hearing is requested by filing a complaint pursuant to §§ 300.507 and 300.508(a) and (b).

(b) Authority of hearing officer.

  (1) A hearing officer under § 300.511 hears, and makes a determination regarding an appeal under paragraph (a) of this section.

  (2) In making the determination under paragraph (b)(1) of this section, the hearing officer may—

    (i) Return the child with a disability to the placement from which the child was removed if the hearing officer determines that the removal was a violation of § 300.530 or that the child's behavior was a manifestation of the child's disability; or

(ii) Order a change of placement of the child with a disability to an appropriate interim alternative educational setting for not more than 45 school days if the hearing officer determines that maintaining the current placement of the child is substantially likely to result in injury to the child or to others.

(3) The procedures under paragraphs (a) and (b)(1) and (2) of this section may be repeated, if the LEA believes that returning the child to the original placement is substantially likely to result in injury to the child or to others.

(c) Expedited due process hearing.

(1) Whenever a hearing is requested under paragraph (a) of this section, the parents or the LEA involved in the dispute must have an opportunity for an impartial due process hearing consistent with the requirements of §§ 300.507 and 300.508(a) through (c) and §§ 300.510 through 300.514, except as provided in paragraph (c)(2) through (4) of this section.

(2) The SEA or LEA is responsible for arranging the expedited due process hearing, which must occur within 20 school days of the date the complaint requesting the hearing is filed. The hearing officer must make a determination within 10 school days after the hearing.

(3) Unless the parents and LEA agree in writing to waive the resolution meeting described in paragraph (c)(3)(i) of this section, or agree to use the mediation process described in § 300.506—

(i) A resolution meeting must occur within seven days of receiving notice of the due process complaint; and

(ii) The due process hearing may proceed unless the matter has been resolved to the satisfaction of both parties within 15 days of the receipt of the due process complaint.

(4) A State may establish different State-imposed procedural rules for expedited due process hearings conducted under this section than it has established for other due process hearings, but, except for the timelines as modified in paragraph (c)(3) of this section, the State must

ensure that the requirements in §§ 300.510 through 300.514 are met.

(5) The decisions on expedited due process hearings are appealable consistent with § 300.514.

(Authority: 20 U.S.C. 1415(k)(3) and (4)(B), 1415(f)(1)(A))

SOURCE: 71 FR 46755, Aug. 14, 2006; 72 FR 17781, April 9, 2007; 80 FR 23666, April 28, 2015, unless otherwise noted.

AUTHORITY: 20 U.S.C. 1221e-3, 1406, 1411–1419, 3474, unless otherwise noted.

Current through March 24, 2016; 81 FR 16051.

| End of Document | © 2016 Thomson Reuters. No claim to original U.S. Government Works. |

n4 Placement During Appeals

Code of Federal Regulations
 Title 34. Education
  Subtitle B. Regulations of the Offices of the Department of Education
   Chapter III. Office of Special Education and Rehabilitative Services, Department of Education
    Part 300. Assistance to States for the Education of Children with Disabilities (Refs & Annos)
     Subpart E. Procedural Safeguards
     Discipline Procedures

34 C.F.R. § 300.533
§ 300.533 Placement during appeals.
Effective: October 30, 2007
Currentness

When an appeal under § 300.532 has been made by either the parent or the LEA, the child must remain in the interim alternative educational setting pending the decision of the hearing officer or until the expiration of the time period specified in § 300.530(c) or (g), whichever occurs first, unless the parent and the SEA or LEA agree otherwise.

(Authority: 20 U.S.C. 1415(k)(4)(A))

Credits

[72 FR 61307, Oct. 30, 2007]

SOURCE: 71 FR 46755, Aug. 14, 2006; 72 FR 17781, April 9, 2007; 80 FR 23666, April 28, 2015, unless otherwise noted.

AUTHORITY: 20 U.S.C. 1221e–3, 1406, 1411–1419, 3474, unless otherwise noted.

Notes of Decisions (2)

Current through March 24, 2016; 81 FR 16051.

| End of Document | © 2016 Thomson Reuters. No claim to original U.S. Government Works. |

n5 Protections for Children Not Determined Eligible for Special Ed

Code of Federal Regulations
  Title 34. Education
    Subtitle B. Regulations of the Offices of the Department of Education
      Chapter III. Office of Special Education and Rehabilitative Services, Department of Education
        Part 300. Assistance to States for the Education of Children with Disabilities (Refs & Annos)
          Subpart E. Procedural Safeguards
            Discipline Procedures

34 C.F.R. § 300.534
§ 300.534 Protections for children not determined eligible for special education and related services.
Effective: October 13, 2006

Currentness

(a) General. A child who has not been determined to be eligible for special education and related services under this part and who has engaged in behavior that violated a code of student conduct, may assert any of the protections provided for in this part if the public agency had knowledge (as determined in accordance with paragraph (b) of this section) that the child was a child with a disability before the behavior that precipitated the disciplinary action occurred.

(b) Basis of knowledge. A public agency must be deemed to have knowledge that a child is a child with a disability if before the behavior that precipitated the disciplinary action occurred—

(1) The parent of the child expressed concern in writing to supervisory or administrative personnel of the appropriate educational agency, or a teacher of the child, that the child is in need of special education and related services;

(2) The parent of the child requested an evaluation of the child pursuant to §§ 300.300 through 300.311; or

(3) The teacher of the child, or other personnel of the LEA, expressed specific concerns about a pattern of behavior demonstrated by the child directly to the director of special education of the agency or to other supervisory personnel of the agency.

(c) Exception. A public agency would not be deemed to have knowledge under paragraph (b) of this section if—

(1) The parent of the child—

(i) Has not allowed an evaluation of the child pursuant to §§ 300.300 through 300.311; or

(ii) Has refused services under this part; or

(2) The child has been evaluated in accordance with §§ 300.300 through 300.311 and determined to not be a child with a disability under this part.

(d) Conditions that apply if no basis of knowledge.

(1) If a public agency does not have knowledge that a child is a child with a disability (in accordance with paragraphs (b) and (c) of this section) prior to taking disciplinary measures against the child, the child may be subjected to the disciplinary measures applied to children without disabilities who engage in comparable behaviors consistent with paragraph (d)(2) of this section.

(2)(i) If a request is made for an evaluation of a child during the time period in which the child is subjected to disciplinary measures under § 300.530, the evaluation must be conducted in an expedited manner.

(ii) Until the evaluation is completed, the child remains in the educational placement determined by school authorities, which can include suspension or expulsion without educational services.

(iii) If the child is determined to be a child with a disability, taking into consideration information from the evaluation conducted by the agency and information provided by the parents, the agency must provide special education and related services in accordance with this part, including the requirements of §§ 300.530 through 300.536 and section 612(a)(1)(A) of the Act.

(Authority: 20 U.S.C. 1415(k)(5))

SOURCE: 71 FR 46755, Aug. 14, 2006; 72 FR 17781, April 9, 2007; 80 FR 23666, April 28, 2015, unless otherwise noted.

AUTHORITY: 20 U.S.C. 1221e–3, 1406, 1411–1419, 3474, unless otherwise noted.

Notes of Decisions (2)

Current through March 24, 2016; 81 FR 16051.

| End of Document | © 2016 Thomson Reuters. No claim to original U.S. Government Works. |

n6 Deferment To and Action By Law Enforcement and Judicial Authorities

Code of Federal Regulations
  Title 34. Education
    Subtitle B. Regulations of the Offices of the Department of Education
      Chapter III. Office of Special Education and Rehabilitative Services, Department of Education
        Part 300. Assistance to States for the Education of Children with Disabilities (Refs & Annos)
          Subpart E. Procedural Safeguards
            Discipline Procedures

34 C.F.R. § 300.535
§ 300.535 Referral to and action by law enforcement and judicial authorities.
Effective: October 13, 2006

Currentness

(a) Rule of construction. Nothing in this part prohibits an agency from reporting a crime committed by a child with a disability to appropriate authorities or prevents State law enforcement and judicial authorities from exercising their responsibilities with regard to the application of Federal and State law to crimes committed by a child with a disability.

(b) Transmittal of records.

(1) An agency reporting a crime committed by a child with a disability must ensure that copies of the special education and disciplinary records of the child are transmitted for consideration by the appropriate authorities to whom the agency reports the crime.

(2) An agency reporting a crime under this section may transmit copies of the child's special education and disciplinary records only to the extent that the transmission is permitted by the Family Educational Rights and Privacy Act.

(Authority: 20 U.S.C. 1415(k)(6))

SOURCE: 71 FR 46755, Aug. 14, 2006; 72 FR 17781, April 9, 2007; 80 FR 23666, April 28, 2015, unless otherwise noted.

AUTHORITY: 20 U.S.C. 1221e–3, 1406, 1411–1419, 3474, unless otherwise noted.

Notes of Decisions (1)

Current through March 24, 2016; 81 FR 16051.

| **End of Document** | © 2016 Thomson Reuters. No claim to original U.S. Government Works. |

n7 Change of Placement Because of Disciplinary Removals Eligible for Special Ed

Code of Federal Regulations
 Title 34. Education
  Subtitle B. Regulations of the Offices of the Department of Education
   Chapter III. Office of Special Education and Rehabilitative Services, Department of Education
    Part 300. Assistance to States for the Education of Children with Disabilities (Refs & Annos)
     Subpart E. Procedural Safeguards
      Discipline Procedures

34 C.F.R. § 300.536
§ 300.536 Change of placement because of disciplinary removals.
Effective: October 13, 2006

Currentness

(a) For purposes of removals of a child with a disability from the child's current educational placement under §§ 300.530 through 300.535, a change of placement occurs if—

(1) The removal is for more than 10 consecutive school days; or

(2) The child has been subjected to a series of removals that constitute a pattern—

(i) Because the series of removals total more than 10 school days in a school year;

(ii) Because the child's behavior is substantially similar to the child's behavior in previous incidents that resulted in the series of removals; and

(iii) Because of such additional factors as the length of each removal, the total amount of time the child has been removed, and the proximity of the removals to one another.

(b)(1) The public agency determines on a case-by-case basis whether a pattern of removals constitutes a change of placement.

(2) This determination is subject to review through due process and judicial proceedings.

(Authority: 20 U.S.C. 1415(k))

SOURCE: 71 FR 46755, Aug. 14, 2006; 72 FR 17781, April 9, 2007; 80 FR 23666, April 28, 2015, unless otherwise noted.

AUTHORITY: 20 U.S.C. 1221e–3, 1406, 1411–1419, 3474, unless otherwise noted.

Notes of Decisions (16)

Current through March 24, 2016; 81 FR 16051.

| **End of Document** | © 2016 Thomson Reuters. No claim to original U.S. Government Works. |

n8 State Enforcement Mechanisms

Code of Federal Regulations
  Title 34. Education
    Subtitle B. Regulations of the Offices of the Department of Education
      Chapter III. Office of Special Education and Rehabilitative Services, Department of Education
        Part 300. Assistance to States for the Education of Children with Disabilities (Refs & Annos)
          Subpart E. Procedural Safeguards
            Discipline Procedures

34 C.F.R. § 300.537
§ 300.537 State enforcement mechanisms.
Effective: October 13, 2006

Currentness

Notwithstanding §§ 300.506(b)(7) and 300.510(d)(2), which provide for judicial enforcement of a written agreement reached as a result of mediation or a resolution meeting, there is nothing in this part that would prevent the SEA from using other mechanisms to seek enforcement of that agreement, provided that use of those mechanisms is not mandatory and does not delay or deny a party the right to seek enforcement of the written agreement in a State court of competent jurisdiction or in a district court of the United States.

(Authority: 20 U.S.C. 1415(e)(2)(F), 1415(f)(1)(B))

SOURCE: 71 FR 46755, Aug. 14, 2006; 72 FR 17781, April 9, 2007; 80 FR 23666, April 28, 2015, unless otherwise noted.

AUTHORITY: 20 U.S.C. 1221e-3, 1406, 1411–1419, 3474, unless otherwise noted.

Current through March 24, 2016; 81 FR 16051.

| End of Document | © 2016 Thomson Reuters. No claim to original U.S. Government Works. |

Made in the USA
San Bernardino, CA
13 April 2017